Trusting Judgements
How to Get the Best out of Experts

Policy- and decision-makers in government and industry constantly face important decisions without full knowledge of all the facts. They rely routinely on expert advice to fill critical gaps in scientific knowledge. There are unprecedented opportunities for experts to influence decisions. Yet even the most experienced can be overconfident and error-prone, and the hidden risk is that scientists and other experts can overreach, often with good intentions, placing more weight on the evidence they provide than is warranted.

This book describes how to identify potentially risky advice, explains why group judgements outperform individual estimates, and provides an accessible and up-to-date guide to the science of expert judgement. Finally, and importantly, it outlines a simple, practical framework that will help policy- and decision-makers to ensure that the advice they receive is relatively reliable and accurate, thus substantially improving the quality of information on which critical decisions are made.

MARK A. BURGMAN is the Adrienne Clarke Chair of Botany at the University of Melbourne and Editor-in-Chief of the journal *Conservation Biology*. He has published over 200 refereed articles and seven authored books in ecology, conservation and risk analysis, and has worked in Australia, the United States and Switzerland. In 2006 he was elected to the Australian Academy of Science and received the Society for Conservation Biology Distinguished Service Award. He won the Royal Society of Victoria Research Medal in 2013.

Trusting Judgements
How to Get the Best out of Experts

MARK A. BURGMAN
Centre of Excellence for Biosecurity Risk Analysis,
School of BioSciences, University of Melbourne

CAMBRIDGE
UNIVERSITY PRESS

University Printing House, Cambridge CB2 8BS, United Kingdom

Cambridge University Press is part of the University of Cambridge.

It furthers the University's mission by disseminating knowledge in the pursuit of education, learning and research at the highest international levels of excellence.

www.cambridge.org
Information on this title: www.cambridge.org/9781107112087

First published 2016

A catalogue record for this publication is available from the British Library

Library of Congress Cataloguing in Publication Data
Burgman, Mark A.
Trusting judgements : how to get the best out of experts / Mark A. Burgman.
    pages   cm
Includes bibliographical references and index.
ISBN 978-1-107-11208-7 (hardback) – ISBN 978-1-107-53102-4 (pbk)
1. Government consultants. 2. Business consultants. 3. Expertise–
Political aspects. 4. Specialists. 5. Public administration–Decision
making. 6. Business–Decision making. I. Title.
JF1525.C6B87 2015
658.4'6–dc23   2015023045

ISBN 978-1-107-11208-7 Hardback
ISBN 978-1-107-53102-4 Paperback

Contents

Preface

This book is intended for people in government, regulatory agencies and business who routinely make decisions and who rely on scientific and technical expertise. So-called evidence-based decision-making has become more popular over the last decade, but often the evidence we need for these decisions is unavailable. Time, money and the pressing nature of many decisions prevent us from collecting much of the information we need. In its place, decision-makers turn to experts to estimate facts or make predictions. The status of scientific and technical experts has evolved over the last 100 years or more to provide unprecedented opportunities for experts to influence decisions. The hidden risk is that scientists and other experts overreach, often with good intentions, placing more weight on the evidence they provide than is warranted. The tendency to overreach is pervasive and more significant than many scientists and decision-makers like to admit. Much of the evidence for these phenomena is drawn from well-established research on decision theory and cognitive psychology. This book documents the extent and importance of this issue, and then outlines a suite of simple, practical tools that will assist decision-makers to make better use of expert estimates and predictions. It provides the means to discriminate good advice from poor, and to help decision-makers to be reasonably and appropriately sceptical. The book promotes a change in attitude towards expert predictions and estimates such that they are treated with the same reverence as data, subjected to the same kinds of cross-examination and verification. By requiring a little discipline from their experts, decision-makers can avoid the most pervasive pitfalls of expert judgements and assure themselves of relatively reliable and accurate expert information.

Acknowledgements

I am grateful to Bill Sutherland, Alan Crowden, Brian Tipping, David Spielgelhalter and Simon French for their guidance, suggestions and encouragement, and to Bill for his hospitality at Cambridge where this was mostly written. Claire Layman, Robin Gregory, Andrew Robinson, Roger Cooke and Anca Hanea provided many detailed and insightful comments. Without them it would be a much worse book. I am especially grateful to John Manger for encouraging me to write this in the first place, and for saying he liked it when it was done. None of this would have been possible without the sustained, creative input of my colleagues in the Centre of Excellence for Biosecurity Risk Analysis at the University of Melbourne and the Intelligence Advanced Research Projects Activity (IARPA) ACE research initiative: Marissa McBride, Steven Mascaro, Brian Manning, Fiona Fidler, Bonnie Wintle, Louisa Flander, Charles Twardy, Neil Thomason and Raquel Ashton. I am grateful for the editorial work of Tracey Hollings, Jess Holliday and David Holliday who created most of the figures. Bonnie Wintle edited the draft manuscript twice, correcting many errors, improving the language, and removing redundant passages. I am also grateful to Janet Walker for her professional editorial polish and advice. This work was supported by the Centre of Excellence for Biosecurity Risk Analysis.

I What's wrong with consulting experts?

I came into the kitchen this morning and the sink was blocked. My wife, who is handier than me, tried the usual things: some drain-cleaning fluid and then a plunger. Despite her enthusiasm for the task, the drain remained blocked. So I rang a plumber. An expert. Someone who has done it before, has the right equipment, and has solved much more difficult drainage problems than were created by my inattention to coffee grounds.

I'm all for the division of labour and specialisation. It's an especially wise strategy for me because I'm one of the world's least handy people. If I need to clear a drain, I call a well-regarded plumber. If I wanted to build a sturdy bridge, I'd contact an engineer who has built lots of bridges. When I needed my knee reconstructed following a bad football tackle, I asked around and found an experienced surgeon with a good reputation.

I'll refer to those expert abilities as skills. Skills are abilities to execute particular tasks efficiently and effectively, acquired through training, concrete practice and feedback.[1] In all these cases, when their actions don't succeed, it's hard for the expert to blame someone else. Their failures are unambiguous and personal. Ideally, you'll be able to look at their records of efficient drain clearing, bridge building and surgical outcomes. Of course, there are shoddy plumbers, reckless engineers and incompetent surgeons. But in the main, they will do a much better job of these things than me.

This book is not about such skills. We also rely on experts for advice when we need to make decisions and we don't have enough information. In government, business and elsewhere, our reliance is greatest when circumstances are unique, the consequences of the decision are significant, the decision is imminent and the future is uncertain. This book deals with the experts on whom we rely for estimation and prediction. Typically, such experts are defined by their qualifications, their experience[2] – and importantly, by their status among their peers. We find someone with the right training and experience, someone whom we trust and can understand.[3] Often, expert judgement is all we have. However, our propensity to turn to experts and accept their judgements uncritically, even when we don't need to, often appears to be automatic, or at least not sufficiently cautious.

This book takes experts to include engineers, political scientists, economists, military and police officers, lawyers and financial analysts, together with the more usual chemists, physicists, geologists, biologists and medical scientists. These people may have many skills. However, their expertise for estimation and prediction is not necessarily supported by relevant, concrete actions and verifiable outcomes. When I use the term 'expert' I will refer to people who are considered by their peers and society at large to have specialist knowledge and who are consulted to make an estimate or prediction. I will show that, in many situations, non-skill-based expertise may not be worth the time and expense involved in using it. While superficially, such expertise may appear to have the same foundations as skill, often it does not.

There is a continuum between skill-based judgement and expert predictions. An engineer's skill may be to design a particular kind of bridge. Circumstances may be such that we consult them on related matters in which they have no direct experience, such as building other kinds of bridges. Beyond that, they may also appear to be expert in more distantly related topics, such as other structures, but have had no exposure to them beyond the things they've seen in textbooks or heard from colleagues. At what point does their ability to estimate or predict become no better than that of a random person from the street? Do they know, themselves, when their knowledge becomes too thin? Do their peers know? We will answer these questions in the chapters that follow.

WHAT DO EXPERTS DO?

Broadly, experts help with three kinds of questions.[4]
They estimate clearly defined, verifiable facts such as:

How prevalent is this disease in the population?
What is the maximum weight this bridge can carry?

They predict events, such as:

Will the President still be in office next year?
How much rain will fall next week?

Quite often, they advise on questions about the best course of action, such as:

What is the best way to manage this problem?
Is this the best portfolio of investments for me?

These are variations on what decision theorist Simon French calls the 'expert problem'.[5] Someone facing a decision consults an expert. The decision-maker alone is responsible for the decision. The emphasis in this book is on how the decision-maker should learn from experts. Sometimes, the experts are also the decision-makers, and sometimes, experts provide information without a decision in mind. I will touch on these issues briefly in the final chapter.

Experts may create models of underlying processes to help them make predictions. For example, many atmospheric scientists, physicists, glaciologists, earth scientists, oceanographers and biologists have been developing models for many years to forecast the outcomes of increasing carbon dioxide in the earth's atmosphere.[6] Their work is the basis for global policy decisions.

When answering questions about verifiable facts, we want the expert to draw on the storehouse of data they have accumulated through training and experience. In the case of predicting outcomes of events, we want them to use models together with their treasure trove of data and experience. We are especially demanding when asking about a course of action because we expect the expert to have data and models on hand and to understand our context and sensitivities. We trust them to have our best interests in mind. We will see, however, that often this is not the case.

The need for experts is felt keenly when it comes to making decisions about the guilt or innocence of people in trials. John Lawson, a lawyer from the University of Missouri, wrote the foundation rules for expert and opinion evidence for the US legal system in 1900. In these rules, opinion is not admissible in evidence except *'on questions of science ...persons instructed therein by study or experience may give their opinions. Such persons are called experts'.*[7] This definition is reiterated in the US Federal Rules of Evidence that state that a witness may qualify as an expert by possessing *'knowledge, skill, experience, training, or education'.*[8] New Federal Rules of Evidence and subsequent decisions broadened the definition to include opinions *'of a type reasonably relied upon by experts in the particular field'.*[9] They must be scientifically reliable (accounting for procedural care and predictive reliability) and grounded in scientific principles and appropriate methodology.[10] All jurisdictions allow expert opinion to inform courts about facts that might be otherwise unattainable because they are future probabilities, contingencies or facts *'not within positive knowledge'.*[11]

Society generally accepts that scientific and technical experts provide a unique, valuable resource. The US National Research Council, for instance, asserted that scientific experts have indispensible knowledge, methodological skills and experience.[12] And scientists themselves believe it. For example, a review of expert veterinary epidemiologists stated *'[e]xperts can be excellent reservoirs, integrators and interpreters of knowledge. In many settings, their ability to generate accurate predictions is a critical function of their profession and a key measure of their success: for example a stock broker's ability to forecast performance of a market, or a physician's ability to triage and assess a patient's need for hospitalization'.*[13] I will examine this general claim as well as the specific performances of

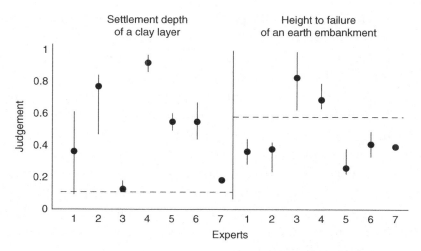

FIGURE 1.1 The correct (measured) value for settlement depth was 1.5 cm and for height to failure was 4.9 m. The y-axis for both was rescaled so the maximum value was 1. Correct values are shown as dashed horizontal lines. The intervals join the 'minimum' and 'maximum' values reported by the experts.

stockbrokers and physicians. In many circumstances, such optimism is misplaced.

SO, WHAT'S THE PROBLEM?

Geophysicist Ellis Krinitzsky spent many years working on earthquake risk, a notoriously difficult scientific problem. In an early review on the reliability of experts, he described an experiment in which seven geotechnical experts predicted the height of fill at which an embankment would fail, and the depth to which sediment would settle.[14] These questions were typical of the kinds of problems geotechnical experts were expected to assess reliably. The experts were provided with the data to make calculations. They used a variety of methods.

The results were not heartening. In Figure 1.1, the dashed lines represent the correct answers to the two questions. The dots are the expert's best guesses. The vertical lines, their uncertainty intervals, connect their 'minimum' and 'maximum' estimates.

There are at least six important things to note about the results of this simple experiment. First, the experts were generally overconfident. They were reasonably sure that the truth lay within the interval shown by the lines connecting their minimum and maximum guesses. However, in the first case, only two people's intervals enclosed the truth. In the second case, no-one's interval enclosed the truth. If their estimates of uncertainty were generally reliable, we would expect most of the intervals to enclose the horizontal dashed lines. Because they did not, it means that, in both cases, the experts were overconfident when they assessed the reliability of their own knowledge.[15]

Second, geophysicists conducted the study in the 1970s. Therefore, technical experts have been aware of these kinds of phenomenon for at least 40 years.

Third, it's possible for everyone to be wrong in the same direction. In the left-hand panel, all the experts overestimated the truth. So, whole groups of experts may be biased.

Fourth, the fact that someone did well on one question does not mean that they will do well on another. Expert 4 did best in the right-hand panel and worst in the left-hand panel.

Fifth, the width of the intervals between the minimum and maximum values tells us how confident the experts were. In the left-hand panel, Expert 3 was confident (the interval was narrow) and accurate (the best guess was close to the truth), whereas Expert 5 was confident and inaccurate. Generally speaking, there was no clear relationship between confidence and accuracy.

Lastly, these were credible, socially accepted experts. They would have passed muster as expert scientists in a court or serving on a government panel dealing with the safety of earth embankments. All were qualified and respected members of scientific societies, attending an international scientific conference. No doubt each had a confident and plausible story to tell about how she or he arrived at an estimate and could defend the interval that she or he gave with the answers.

Misjudgements such as those reflected in these geophysicists' academic estimates may seem relatively benign, but experts' mistakes may have more direct consequences. Fingerprint identification is based on expert judgement. Is it reliable?

In May 1997, an officer of the Boston Police Department was shot twice following a struggle with an assailant. The assailant ran, leaving behind the baseball hat he was wearing. He entered a nearby home, where he stopped to drink a glass of water. He then fled, leaving the gun, the sweatshirt he had been wearing and a thumbprint on the glass.[16]

The injured police officer later identified Stephan Cowans (Figure 1.2) from a photo array and then from a live line-up. The family in the house did not identify him. A fingerprint expert, however, matched the thumbprint to Cowans'. Having served six years in a Massachusetts prison, he was released in 2004 after the fingerprint evidence on which he had been convicted was contradicted by new DNA evidence.

Cowans' case is not unique. In March 2004, bombs exploded in the commuter train system in Madrid, killing 191 people. Brandon Mayfield, a US lawyer, was incorrectly identified from fingerprints taken from the crime scene.[17] Despite three FBI examiners and an

FIGURE 1.2 Stephan Cowans listening to testimony, prior to being convicted and spending five and a half years in Massachusetts prisons.
Source: *Boston Herald*, Boston, MA.[18]

external expert agreeing on the identification, Spanish authorities eventually matched the prints to another suspect.

So how reliable is fingerprint evidence? The earliest large-scale study I found on the reliability of print examiners' decisions was published in 2011 in the prestigious journal *Proceedings of the National Academy of Sciences of the USA*.[19] The study gave pairs of fingerprints to 169 experts and asked them to determine whether the same person had made them, or not. A total of 32 per cent of the pairs were 'mated' pairs (from the same people) and 68 per cent were 'un-mated'.

The false-positive rate (the chance that fingerprint experts would falsely conclude two prints were the same) was satisfyingly low, at 0.1 per cent. The false-negative rate (the chance of falsely declaring two prints were different when in fact they were from the same person) was higher, at 7.5 per cent. A substantial number of the comparisons were judged by the experts to be 'inconclusive' or of no value. It is important to note that the experts knew they were being tested. We could reasonably assume that people unaware of such scrutiny may perform differently.

A UK-based study asked 27 experts to make a total of 2,484 judgements about pairs of fingerprints.[20] A quarter were controls, similar to the US-based study above. In the others, the experts were told fictitious emotional background stories that included murder and personal attacks, or they were shown disturbing photographs purportedly coming from the crime scenes from which the finger-prints were taken. Participants were not given the option of making inconclusive judgements. They had to decide either 'match' or 'no match'.

People were more likely to find a match between ambiguous fin-gerprints (an example is shown in Figure 1.3) if they had been exposed to emotional background stories or photographs. Participants found matches in 47 per cent of cases without emotional stimulus and in 58 per cent of cases when their emotions had been stirred.

This tells us that how we feel influences how we make technical judgements. In many circumstances, the people making judgements about fingerprints are aware of the background, and therefore may be susceptible to emotional distortions. Something as seemingly straightforward as judging fingerprints is error-prone and easily biased.[21] The prospects are not good for other situations in which experts are asked to make more difficult assessments in emotionally charged circumstances.

Expert misjudgements may have global consequences. As late as 2006, the International Monetary Fund (IMF) claimed that modern financial systems made the world a safer place. Their report on financial stability trumpeted the very instruments that led soon afterwards to global catastrophic financial collapse. It said, '*[i]n particular, the emergence of numerous, and often very large, institutional investors and the rapid growth of credit risk transfer instruments have enabled banks to manage their credit risk more actively and to outsource the warehousing of credit risk to a diverse range of investors. A wider dispersion of credit risk has "derisked" the banking*

FIGURE 1.3 Example of an 'ambiguous' pair of fingerprints.
Source: Dror et al. (2005). The author of the paper from which the image is sourced used a low-quality image to emphasise some of the real difficulties in matching prints.[22]

sector'.[23] Very few financial analysts saw the collapse coming. Most analysts at the time agreed with the IMF experts that the new financial systems were safe, well regulated and stable.

Less than two years later, in 2007, the system failed (Figure 1.4). Lest we forget, investment banks began to write down billions of dollars in mortgage-backed derivatives and other so-called toxic securities. In the US, Bear Stearns collapsed, Fannie Mae and Freddie Mac were taken over by the federal government, Lehman Brothers fell, Merrill Lynch was sold, AIG was saved, and a US$700 billion bailout bill was rushed into law.[24] The risks taken by the largest banks and investment firms in much of the Western world were so *excessive and foolhardy* that they threatened to bring down the financial system itself.[25]

Emotion and context may affect financial analysts and forensic scientists, but are other kinds of scientists immune? In the late 1990s, sociologist Lisa Campbell interviewed marine biologists and conservation experts and asked if they thought marine turtles could be

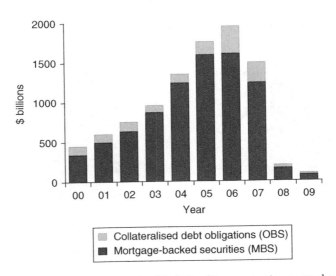

FIGURE 1.4 From economist Mark Zandi's 2010 testimony to the Financial Crisis Inquiry Commission. Securitisation occurred when banks and other financial institutions packaged various types of loan (including mortgages) into securities and sold them to global investors.[26]

harvested sustainably.[27] She found a range of answers, from *'maybe; let's learn by trying'* (the fisheries model) to *'no, under no circumstances'*. If you have ever discussed the topic of sustainable harvesting with marine biologists you'll know to expect a range of answers.

The positions were based on different kinds of evidence. Proponents of sustainable use were influenced by international conventions and local customs. They saw the potential to learn about the system by monitoring and valued conservation incentives arising from improved economic status. Opponents of sustainable use were influenced by a lack of faith in free-market economics. They raised many moral and philosophical arguments against the use of wildlife (Figure 1.5).

Campbell asked each expert an additional, fascinating question regarding whether they thought their opinion was objective and evidence-based, and whether the opinions of those who disagreed with them were value-laden. Most of the experts saw opposing views as influenced by 'emotions'. They claimed dispassionate scientific objectivity for their own views, irrespective of their positions. Experts couched their arguments in scientific terms, downplaying the roles of other values. Five experts felt that nonscientific 'conservationists' without training were emotional about turtles, while they themselves were not. Those who opposed consumptive use characterised their opponents as greedy and exploitative. Campbell noted that since there are so few certainties in marine turtle conservation science, experts do not have to engage with the science-based arguments of their opponents. Most scientists wrongly assume that training protects people from emotional investment in their subject material.

Motivational bias – which I describe further in Chapter 3 – is the intentional or unintentional adjustment of an estimate or prediction attributable to values or prospects for reward.[28,29] Scientists' values imbue their technical judgements. Marine biologists are no more deluded than are other kinds of scientists. In fact, it is commonplace for experts to be unaware that they are influenced by values and context.

FIGURE 1.5 Marine turtles are iconic or 'charismatic' fauna which attract considerable attention from conservationists. Internationally, there is debate over indigenous harvesting of marine turtles and other marine fauna of conservation significance. Source: iStockphoto.com.

Scientists are taught to believe in the objectivity of the scientific method. They find it difficult to imagine that another scientifically trained, equally clever person, who has access to the same data and models, could come to a different conclusion. Scientists are credible because they believe in their own objectivity.

When scientists rate different types of evidence, often they assign expert judgement to the bottom rung and direct observations to the top.[30] Despite this, expert estimates and predictions arise with pervasive regularity in almost all areas of applied science. If decision-making were an entirely objective, detached scientific process that led inexorably to a single, rational outcome, finding and using experts would not be problematic. Ideally, there would be a pool of people with appropriate qualifications, extensive experience and sound technical skills that we could call on to estimate or predict in a consistent manner.

Unfortunately this is rarely, if ever, the case. Decisions involve both facts and values. Values are statements about what we want or what we think is important.[31] Estimates and predictions are statements about quantities and events. They describe the conditions of a system or the outcomes of actions[32] that could be verified with independent information, at least in theory.

Despite this superficially simple discrimination, facts and values are deeply intertwined. Facts are uncertain and are often imbued with values, perceptions and emotions, as we saw in the earlier example where fingerprint judgements were biased by emotional priming. Moreover, there is no single, right way of assessing values. Nor are experts entirely objective and independent.[33] In most practical situations, the pool of potential experts is small, composed of people with differing values and partially overlapping experiences.[34] And some experts are just incompetent. We should worry about them as we might about a potentially shoddy plumber or incompetent surgeon, but without the comfort of a track record.

Values are inescapable also because the consequences of decisions are inherently value-laden. For example, all human lives may be equal under the law, but the importance of different kinds of fatality depends on your point of view. Psychologist Paul Slovic gave the example that society may be best served by minimising the number of worker deaths per tonne of coal produced, whereas a union representative is obliged to minimise the number of deaths per worker per year.[35] These different objectives may lead to appreciably different safety strategies, yet both are ethically justifiable.

Similarly, the death of a young person elicits a stronger social reaction than the death of an old person. On-the-job mortality risk (i.e. not counting age-related mortality from heart attacks and the like) increases with age in virtually every industry. Thus, the average 60-year-old manufacturing worker is 80 per cent more likely to die from work-related accidents than the average 30-year-old, and men are much more likely than women to die in accidents at work.[36] Such discrepancies are socially acceptable.

Motivational biases arise even in highly technical areas. When the NASA space shuttle *Challenger* (Figure 1.6) exploded soon after launch in 1986, the public wondered how it could have happened. After all, the schoolteacher Christa McAuliffe, who died on board the rocket together with the astronauts, had been told the risk of a failure was one in 100,000 launches. Up to that point, there had been only about 100 launches of the two space shuttles, and there had been no failures.

Physicist Richard Feynman was part of a team that investigated the accident. He reported[37] the range safety engineer had studied for all previous unmanned rocket flights and found that, out of a total of nearly 2,900 flights, 121 had failed (one in 25). The engineer noted that, with special safety systems, a figure of below one in 100 might be achieved – but that even *'1 in 1,000 is probably not attainable with today's technology'*. More recent studies suggest that failure probabilities, especially early in the program, were much higher than one in 100.[38]

FIGURE 1.6 NASA Space Shuttle *Challenger* lifts off on its maiden flight, 4 April 1983.[39] Source: Getty Images.

This estimate was in stark contrast to Feynman's record of the NASA managers who believed that, since the shuttle was a manned vehicle, *'the probability of mission success is necessarily very close to 1.0'.*[40] That is, managers believed that the probability of failure *should* be as low as one in 100,000. They could estimate this level of safety only by ignoring their own records that showed difficulties, near-accidents and accidents, all giving warning that the probability of flight failure was not so very small. Feynman concluded, *'It would appear that, for whatever purpose, ..., the management of NASA exaggerates the reliability of its product, to the point of fantasy'.*[41] NASA managers had a vested interest in a safe system and convinced themselves, and others, that it was so, despite the data. In hindsight, we can see that there were 135 missions in the space shuttle program between 1981 and 2011, and two catastrophic failures, much closer to the safety engineer's assessment than to NASA management's estimate.

WE RELY ON EXPERT JUDGEMENT, EVEN WHEN WE SHOULDN'T

Interestingly, our propensity to ignore evidence is quite pervasive. In 1954, psychologist Paul Meehl published a book that reviewed about 20 studies comparing the clinical diagnoses of doctors to the predictions of simple statistical models (Figure 1.7).[42] It may surprise you to learn that the diagnostic error rate in clinical medicine in most fields is roughly 10–15 per cent.[43] These 20 studies, when combined, showed an overwhelming preponderance of results in favour of statistical over clinical judgement.

For instance, Meehl described the earliest study he could find that compared clinical estimates with quantitative prediction.[44] In the study, published in 1928 by the Illinois State Parole Board, a sociologist scored the characteristics and parole success or failure of 3,000 criminal offenders. The sociologist scored 21 factors for each criminal (including the crime, the sentence, their age, number of previous offences, and so on) and then simply counted the number of 'favourable' and 'unfavourable' factors in each case. Three prison

(a)

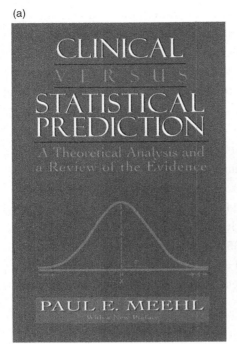

(b)

FIGURE 1.7 Paul Everett Meehl (1920–2003).
Source: www.tc.umn.edu.au/~pemeehl.

psychiatrists also made subjective clinical judgements. The index and the psychiatrists were about equally accurate at predicting parole success, but the psychiatrists were inferior at predicting failure.[45] Meehl suggested that it is in the interests of patients for clinicians to use quantitative approaches routinely, to reduce the number of false diagnoses. Although numerous studies have shown that psychiatrists cannot reliably predict who is dangerous,[46] most courts accept expert diagnoses.

Meehl's book caused a controversy[47] that is still not resolved. It was very confronting for clinicians to be told that a simple statistical model would make fewer mistakes than an experienced professional.

Meehl and his colleagues repeated the analysis in 1996.[48] They found 136 medical and mental health studies comparing clinical and statistical prediction.[49] Yet, despite decades of consistent research findings in favour of the statistical method,[50] most professionals continue to use subjective, clinical judgements and do not use quantitative tools, even when they are available.[51] In their 2008 review[52] of clinical misdiagnoses, medical administrator Eta Berner and physician Mark Graber noted, '[d]ecision-support tools have the potential to improve care and decrease variations in care delivery, but, unfortunately, clinicians disregard them, even in areas where care is known to be suboptimal and the support tool is well integrated into their workflow'.

The superiority of simple models over expert judgement is not unique to medicine. Lawyer Theodore Ruger and his colleagues[53] began with 628 cases previously decided by the US Supreme Court. They developed a statistical model based on six attributes:

1. the circuit of origin for the case;
2. the issue area of the case;
3. the type of petitioner (e.g. the United States, an injured person, an employer);
4. the type of respondent;
5. the ideological direction of the lower court ruling; and
6. whether or not the petitioner argued the constitutionality of a law or practice.

They applied this model to 68 new cases and predicted the outcomes.

They then consulted 83 experts. All had written and taught, practised before, and/or clerked at the Supreme Court. They comprised 71 academics and 12 appellate attorneys.

The model did better at predicting the outcomes of Supreme Court decisions, even though the model and the experts were about equally reliable in predicting the opinions of individual judges. The model got it right in 75 per cent of cases, whereas the consensus position of the lawyers got it right in 59 per cent of the cases.

The authors had expected the experts would do better at predicting Supreme Court decisions, and they commented: '*[w]ith our skepticism significantly dispelled, we now shift from speculating how a machine that is blinded to doctrinal, textual, and procedural particularity would do poorly at predicting cases, to asking why it did so well'*.[54]

With evidence increasingly supporting the use of 'machines' as decision-support tools, it was only a matter of time before they were integrated into major sports. Unsurprisingly, this also met with resistance. A company called QuesTec designed a camera system in the 1990s to track the trajectory of a baseball. They marketed the idea of improving umpires' decisions. Major League Baseball took up the initiative in 2001. The umpires and players resisted for two main reasons. First, they were concerned that the system may be inaccurate. Second, given that it was set up initially in only a few baseball parks, umpiring would not have been consistent. The umpires went as far as taking legal action to have the system removed.

The controversy peaked when pitcher Curt Schilling (Figure 1.8) used a bat to smash one of QuesTec's field cameras after he disagreed with the technical judgements, an act that led to a fine for the pitcher. Official resistance to the new technology was dropped as part of the contract negotiations after the 2005 season, ending the legal challenges. Statistics accumulated, and it is now clear that, with the assistance of feedback from the technology, umpires are more likely to correctly identify pitches that are outside the width of the plate, too high or too low.[55]

The urge to believe our instinctive judgements is powerful, even when we are aware of their frailties. Psychologist Daniel Kahneman had read Meehl's book when, in the 1950s, he got a job assessing new recruits to the Israeli army and deciding who would make a good officer.[56] The system involved having groups of eight recruits carry a pole over a wall without it touching the ground or the wall itself. If the group failed, they had to repeat the job. It was a hot, unpleasant and difficult task. Kahneman observed who helped and

FIGURE 1.8 Pitcher Curt Schilling of the Boston Red Sox.
Source: Getty Images.

who was lazy. He noted who was dominant and who listened, who became disgruntled when their ideas weren't used, and so on. On the basis of these observations, he formed opinions about who would make the best leaders.

Disarmingly, Kahneman remembers that the statistical evidence should have shaken his confidence in his judgements of particular candidates, but it did not. He knew that his subjective and unstructured observations were of no value in predicting who would make the best officers, but he continued to feel and act as if each particular prediction was valid. He was reminded of visual illusions, which remain compelling even when you know that what you see is false, and coined the term the *'illusion of validity'*.

Physicist and statistician Freeman Dyson had a similar experience during World War II.[57] He was given the job of analysing the operational performance of the British Bomber Command. Everyone at Bomber Command saw bomber crews as tightly knit teams of seven, with the gunners playing an essential role defending their comrades against fighter attack, while the pilots flew an irregular corkscrew to defend them against flak. They believed that, as they became more skilful and more closely bonded, their chances of survival improved. This belief was essential for morale. The survival rate for bombing teams to reach the end of a 30-operation tour was just 25 per cent. They needed to believe that there was benefit if they improved their skills. Dyson analysed the data and found that whether a crew lived or died was purely a matter of chance. Their belief in the life-saving effect of experience was an illusion.

THE CAUSE OF THE RELIANCE

With all these examples available to us, why do we – as both experts and decision-makers – persist in ignoring evidence and rely on subjective predictions, even when demonstrably better data-driven and model-based assessments are available? After all, neither patients nor doctors want doctors to use statistical tools. People listen to political pundits, scientists and financial advisers, despite the data.

Meehl[58] suggested that experts are motivated to ignore data through fear of becoming redundant. Experts value esteem and status. Consider how unhappy senior partners in a law firm would be, says Meehl, to learn that paralegals with a few years of experience could predict the opinions of an appellate court as accurately as a partner. Experts often hold a fondness for a personal theory. Mathematical prediction is often seen as dehumanising, especially for people who lack experience with quantitative methods.

From the perspective of the user of expert advice, it may be that it is mentally difficult to make carefully reasoned decisions. We tend to 'off-load' the effort – including that of using a decision-support tool – to someone we believe is better equipped to perform the task.[59]

Forecasting specialist Scott Armstrong speculated[60] that many decision-makers want to avoid responsibility. A decision-maker who calls in the best available expert can blame the expert if the forecasts are inaccurate.[61]

Another reason for our dependence on experts may lie in a deep-rooted human need to believe that certainty exists, and that we just need to consult the right oracle to discover it. Society creates hierarchies of technical and scientific status that pander to this need.[62] These edifices resist data and criticism and generate self-fulfilling pronouncements.

SCIENTIFIC AUTHORITY

A key problem, and one of the central themes of this book, is that scientific experts often assume a position of authority, reinforced by professional status. It can intimidate people who wish to examine expert opinions critically, leading to a culture of technical control in which expert opinions are rarely challenged successfully,[63] let alone cross-examined or verified. For instance, the Supreme Court of Canada noted that expert opinion *'dressed up in scientific language'* may appear *'virtually infallible'*.[64]

When an expert estimates an 'objective' fact they provide a statement based on available information, overlain by morals, values and beliefs, and filtered through personal experience. They may also consult friends and colleagues, information in books, papers and reports. They dredge information from these sources and combine it in unstructured ways. Uncertainty allows different opinions to emerge. Advocacy groups take advantage of this uncertainty to select experts whose position is sympathetic to a social position. They use the expert's authority to influence decisions in government, courts and other institutions.

Science reinforces obedience to authority[65] in a number of ways. Those who dispute scientific opinion may be dismissed as people who do not think rationally. Scientific argument may be out of reach to non-experts.[66] It is often difficult to distinguish data from expert opinion in databases and official reports. Assessments may become too complex and daunting to be challenged.

Accordingly, philosopher Douglas Walton claimed that an argument from authority is improper when '[t]here is a naked assertion that the identity of the expert warrants acceptance of the proposal'.[67] Irrefutable, unspecified wisdom and unassailable expert status generate a culture of technical control. Scientist Mary O'Brien argued similarly that expert assessments provide a mechanism for a technocratic subset of society to impose their values on the rest of society.[68] While both of these writers defend science and realism, both argue that expert authority is legitimate only if it can be challenged.

These comments on scientific authority suggest that what counts as expertise depends on context. If experts are tested, then expertise from all domains may be considered, including what may be considered lay knowledge.[69] Still, it is commonplace for those regarded as 'non-experts' to be left out of the conversation, often to the detriment of the decision. For example, decision analyst Lee Failing and her colleagues noted in dealing with water-resource decisions in British Columbia that many people with relevant technical knowledge are mistakenly excluded from environmental decisions.[70]

EXPERTS AND ADVOCATES

In many situations, experts act as advocates. It may be that they advocate a scientific position based on an accepted range of data and methodologies. They may do so on behalf of a client, such as a proponent of a particular project or decision. Advocacy is especially strident when issues are emotionally or politically charged.

Salmon in Canada and the Pacific north west of the United States are economically, socially and culturally valuable. People have strong opinions about them. Declines in wild salmon populations may have been caused by habitat degradation, dams, harvesting, fish hatcheries, el Niño events, predation and invasion of exotic organisms. Experts disagree about the causes of decline. Data are often unavailable or equivocal. Recovery teams are composed of people with technical backgrounds, and yet, biologist Mary Ruckelshaus noted: '*Major technical disagreements stemming from philosophical differences that seem to run as deep as religious beliefs are commonplace in such technical teams.*'[71]

Lawyer and psychologist Dan Kahan has observed the same phenomenon in debates about climate change and biological evolution. He finds that people adopt a position, often one that accords with the views of their peers or their social context, and then select scientific arguments to defend that position. A person's scientific or technical training does not protect them from this kind of post hoc rationalisation. If anything, technical training only serves to help them to use selective scientific evidence more effectively. Kahan notes, '*Those whose cultural commitments predispose them to be concerned about climate change become even more so as their level of science comprehension increases. Those whose commitments predispose them to be less concerned become all the more skeptical.*'[72]

It is unconventional in science to admit that experts are advocates. In fact, when people look for experts, they often look for 'impartial' contributors. For example, a facility for the storage of high-level nuclear wastes[73] was proposed at Yucca Mountain in Nevada. The site would need to store radioactive material for 10,000 years. To evaluate the question of how likely it is that magma will intrude into the facility, releasing damaging radiation, the project leader chose ten expert earth scientists. He selected them on the basis of their expertise, institutional affiliations and 'normative qualities'. These included their ability to communicate, interpersonal skills, flexibility and impartiality. These attributes were not defined or reported, but instead were interpreted subjectively by the group leader.

They settled on an estimate of 1/10,000, with an uncertainty range of 5/1,000,000 to 5/10,000. The report claimed the result '...*cut through the miasma of scientific discord about volcanoes around Yucca Mountain...'.*[74] Other scientists saw the process as simply confirming the beliefs of those who were predisposed to think the proposal was safe.[75]

Such unstructured expert selection processes are the norm. They are more likely to result in biased estimates than stratified selection processes. I argue that impartial experts are simply those whose interests are uncontroversial or undeclared.

In adversarial legal systems, potential expert witnesses are selected overwhelmingly for their credentials and for the strength of their support for the lawyer's viewpoint. Lawyers search for appropriate attributes in an expert and develop strategies to maximise their chance of winning a case.[76] A close association between a lawyer and an expert may orientate the expert's opinion to provide greatest benefit for the person who retains them. Success often depends on the plausibility or self-confidence of the expert, rather than on the expert's professional competence.[77]

While some bias is inevitable in adversarial systems – because experts are paid and instructed by one party – the system encourages critical questioning of expert evidence. Biases may be counteracted by the ability of courts and opposing lawyers to cross-examine, but it has limits.

In courts, difficulties in dealing with advocates have led to other models. Witness conferencing involves the confrontation of two teams of experts, allowing simultaneous, joint hearing of expert evidence.[78] Users of this system claim that it is efficient; it clarifies technical issues and elicits expert opinions relatively reliably. A court may direct experts to confer and develop a consensus position. It may also appoint a specialist to assist the court. In the latter case, if the expert's opinion is not questioned, the information may be believed simply because of the status of the person providing it. If you've read the rest of this chapter, alarm bells will be ringing by now.

WHERE DOES THIS LEAVE US?

I have described some possible causes of our unreasonable reliance on experts. I have argued that there are circumstances where we should afford more weight to data and statistical models. But such tools may not be available. In their absence, expert opinion is unavoidable. So where should we go from here?

To make the best use of experts, we need to rethink our attitudes towards them. Scientists consider it to be unconscionable to manipulate data. It is unethical to weight data arbitrarily or filter them to suit personal goals. In stark contrast, we know that expert estimates are prey to strong social and psychological forces that lead to weighting and filtering. Yet we do virtually nothing about it.

The aim of this book is to promote a reverence for expert estimates and predictions akin to that for data. That is, we should use repeatable and evidence-based methods to acquire expert estimates. We should strive to avoid bias and error. We should test methods for acquiring expert estimates, validate expert predictions, and adjust accordingly as we learn about them.

For any given decision, the following questions then arise. How is expert status decided and validated? Who qualifies as an expert? Are their estimates any good? How can we find ways to improve their reliability and accuracy? I hope to satisfy the aim of this book by outlining a few general tools that may be useful in answering these questions. It does not deal with the more complex tasks of forecasting dynamic systems, undertaking foresight activities, or making policy recommendations. Other methods, guidelines and commentaries are available for those.[79] The relatively narrow domain of estimating quantities and predicting events is challenging enough.

You may have been left with the impression that I cherry-picked examples in which experts have done poorly. I wish that were the case, but it is not. I've presented some of this material from time to time to professional audiences. I've met engineers, doctors and conservation biologists alike who deny that these things happen. Some become angry when we question the validity of untested expert assessments or the status of revered specialists. It is difficult to contemplate that unaided expert opinion might be error-prone, overconfident and riddled with values and emotional responses. For this reason, I've spent years looking for professional domains in which experts involved in estimation and prediction are reliable. As we will see in the next chapters, they exist, but they are in the minority.

2 Kinds of uncertainty

Before examining expert estimates and predictions more carefully, we first need to understand uncertainty so that we can recognise how experts deal with it (or not, as the case may be). Uncertainty is the pervasive unpredictability that obscures and shapes our view of the world.

All expert estimates involve a mixture of different kinds of uncertainty. Not all of them can be quantified, and few are usually acknowledged. Even quantified uncertainty comes in different forms. One useful classification[1] of ideas about uncertainty distinguishes natural (aleatory) variation, knowledge-based (epistemic) uncertainty and language-based (linguistic) uncertainty.

Natural variation is naturally occurring, unpredictable change, differences attributable to 'true' heterogeneity. For instance, the temperature of water in a stream varies from instant to instant and from place to place, so that there is no, single, precise value that summarises completely the stream's temperature. This is the domain of statistics and conventional scientific training.

Knowledge-based uncertainty exists because of the limitations of our knowledge about a fact. Measurement devices are inaccurate. There are insufficient data. We are forced to guess about unknown circumstances and to provide subjective estimates of statistical attributes.

Language-based uncertainty arises because natural language is imprecise. Words can have more than one meaning. Meaning may be vague, or it may depend on context, and yet the context is not provided. It results from people using words differently or inexactly.

I treat the ideas about natural, knowledge-based and language-based uncertainty in detail below. These concepts have

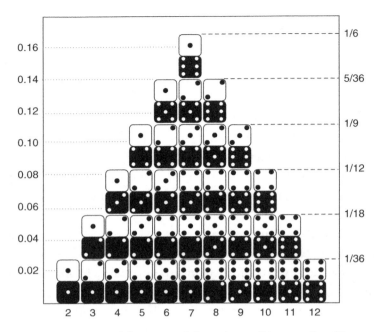

FIGURE 2.1 The different possibilities from rolling two dice. The y-axes give the chances of rolling each of the numbers 2 through 12, expressed as probabilities (left) and frequencies (right).
Source: after http://stungeye.com/archive/by_date/2013/12/17.

their roots in ideas of uncertainty that arose in thinking about dice, cards and the chances of winning a lottery. When philosophers and mathematicians began to wrestle with uncertainty they were trying to estimate the probability of winning games of chance. Classical, objective probability is a measure representing *'the proportion of equally probable cases'*, a concept attributed to Gerolamo Cardan, a sixteenth-century mathematician and gambler.[2] The idea was to explain long-run relative frequencies of events. For example, of the 36 possible results of throwing two dice, three give a total of 10 (5 + 5, 4 + 6, 6 + 4), so the probability of throwing a 10 is 1/12 (3/36).

While probability can be viewed as the relative frequency with which an event is expected to occur, as in the frequency with which we expect 10 to turn up when rolling two dice (Figure 2.1), it can also be viewed as the degree of belief warranted by evidence, such as the chance you give to your team winning a game of football. This important duality is a critical element in understanding and using expert judgements.

It is interesting to note that lawyer John Lawson's view in 1900 was that expert judgement is more akin to belief than relative frequency. He stated, '*[t]he witness swears as to the present conviction of his own mind as to an actual fact*'.[3] The idea that a probability can be a belief also appears in engineering. In a 1993 paper on systems safety, Stephens and colleagues suggested that probability be defined as '*the degree of belief, held by the person providing the information*'.[4] Similarly, in a quantitative risk analysis conducted in 1981, Kaplan and Garrick defined probability as '*a numerical measure of a state of knowledge, a degree of belief, a state of confidence*'.[5]

When the concept of probability relates to an event which, when repeated, occurs with a certain frequency, it describes a chance process. It is objective in the sense that it exists, independently of our knowledge of it. For example, the probability of failure of a dam wall may be known (within some uncertainty limits) because there have been many such walls built and because physical characteristics and failure rates are known from theory and measurement. The concept is equivalent to the chance of rolling a given number when playing a dice game.

The dual nature of probability was recognised in texts dating from the 1660s, including the first influential text on probability, the *Port Royal Logic*, written in 1662 by Pierre Nicole and Antoine Arnauld. Parts of this book are attributed to their colleague, philosopher and mathematician, Blaise Pascal.[6] Pascal had been writing to his colleague, Fermat, discussing the correct way to divide up the stakes between gamblers when a game was interrupted before it was concluded. The problem was about long-run frequencies.

The book suggested that probabilities for things other than games of chance should be judged objectively based on past frequencies. Thus, for example, Pascal advised that we should not be too

Table 2.1 *Pascal's wager*

	State of the universe	
A person's life	*God exists*	*God does not exist*
Pious	Eternal bliss	Loss of worldly enjoyment
Worldly	Eternal damnation	Worldly enjoyment

afraid of death by lightning strike because it *'is very uncommon (reportedly less than one in two million)'*.[7] He used the word *'probability'* freely in place of the word *'chance'*.

The other side of the probabilistic coin is concerned with reasonable degrees of belief. It applies when a probability is unknown or unknowable. Pascal wrote about the reason why people should believe in God. It became known as Pascal's wager. Pascal reasoned that either (a) God exists, or (b) God does not exist. Somewhat independently, people choose either to live (a) a 'worldly' life, or (b) a 'pious' life. We can put his reasoning into a table (see Table 2.1).

The 'pay-offs' a person receives are shaded in Table 2.1. They depend on the state of the universe and on a person's choice about how he or she lives. Pascal argued that if a person believes that God might exist, no matter how small the probability, the tradeoff is so extreme that one should lead a pious life. This was an early example of a subjective probability used in a rational argument.

Subjective probabilities are expected to follow the rules of probability. They should be *answerable* to frequencies in the sense that frequency data should influence estimates when they are known.[8] For example, if I believe that the chance that an oil spill will eliminate a bird rookery is 70 per cent, the chance that it will not eliminate the rookery should be 30 per cent.

Statements about probability may include linguistic uncertainty, such as borderline cases or ambiguities, so that it may be hard to know what a statement means. In the 1960s, intelligence analysts in the US were developing protocols to communicate their predictions about geopolitical events with senior staff. History professor and analyst Sherman Kent was assisting them. He said once to a fellow analyst, '*[b]y the way, what did you people mean by the expression "serious possibility"? What kind of odds did you have in mind? I told him that my personal estimate was ... around 65 to 35 in favor of an attack. He was somewhat jolted by this; he and his colleagues had read "serious possibility" to mean odds very considerably lower. ... It was another jolt to find that each Board member had had somewhat different odds in mind and the low man was thinking of about 20 to 80, the high of 80 to 20. The rest ranged in between'.*[9]

A proposition may be stated in probabilistic terms, but there may be no underlying fact. That is, statements may have frequency interpretations, but the assignment of a probability may be subjective. Understanding what is meant may not depend on repeated trials. For example, the following circumstances do not require repetition to be understood:

- The Tasmanian Tiger is probably extinct;
- Living in this city, you will probably learn to like football; or
- My brother is probably sleeping at this moment.

For instance, I can say that my brother is probably sleeping just because I know he is lazy. Equally reasonably, the statements may have a frequency interpretation. In support of the assertion that my brother is sleeping at this time, I could sample days and times randomly. I could build up a reliable picture of his sleeping habits from records of my brother's behaviour, and eventually, after making some assumptions, report a probability that he is, in fact, sleeping.

'Bayesian' statisticians use subjective probabilities (degrees of belief, such as 'I believe that my brother is asleep') whereas 'frequentist' statisticians see probabilities as relative frequencies (such as 'at this time of day, he is asleep nine times out of ten'). Subjective probabilities can be updated via Bayes' theorem when new data come to hand. In most cases, repeated application of Bayes' theorem results in subjective probabilities that converge on objective chance. And there are objective ways to arrive at subjective probabilities, including the use of betting behaviour.[10] We revisit this question in a later chapter.

Prior to the 1660s the word 'probable' was evaluative.[11] If something was probable, it was worth doing (my sleeping brother would appreciate this definition). It also meant trustworthy. A probable doctor was a trusted one. Jesuit theologians in the period before 1660 used the term 'probable' to mean 'approved by the wise', propositions supported by testimony or some authorised opinion. These meanings are like the terms 'belief' and 'credibility', and allowed that a proposition could be both probable (because it is made by a trustworthy person) and false.[12]

Inductive reasoning developed from medical diagnosis and the related 'low' sciences of alchemists, astrologers and miners who relied on empirical evidence to guide them to explanations.[13] It arose in parallel with ideas about probability and led to the rise of reasoning from observed effects to hypothetical causes. One can have partial belief in several different explanations but only one of them will be true.

NATURAL VARIATION AND LACK OF KNOWLEDGE

As we noted above, natural variation is naturally occurring, unpredictable change, differences attributable to 'true' heterogeneity. Generally, we also lack knowledge about parameters or models, and measurements are error prone. Measurement error results in (apparently) random variation in repeated measurements arising from the accuracy of the equipment and the skill of the observer. For example, there have been many attempts to estimate the speed of light (Figure 2.2). Theory tells us that there is, in fact, a single value. The intervals around the point estimates represent variability in the measuring equipment. Clearly, the intervals associated with each measurement in Figure 2.2 did not capture all uncertainty. For instance, many intervals do not overlap the intervals associated with

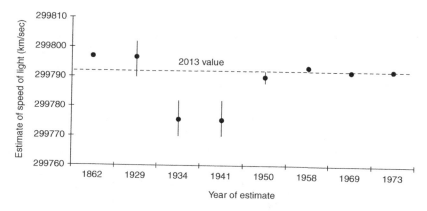

FIGURE 2.2 Measurements of the speed of light together with reported uncertainties (confidence intervals) for the period 1862–1973, compared to the current (2013) estimate. Source: adapted from Henrion and Fischhoff (1986) in Morgan and Henrion (1990).[14]

measurements made subsequently. The differences include variations among experimental protocols, people and equipment, as well as variability in measuring equipment.

Lack of knowledge also includes systematic error that is not (apparently) random. It can result from a decision to exclude (or include) data that ought not to be excluded (or included). It can result from consistent, unintentional errors in calibrating equipment or recording measurements.

For example, when levels of soot in the atmosphere rise, more people die from heart and lung disease. In 1997, the US Environmental Protection Agency (EPA) limited permissible levels of pollutants, in part based on the results of statistical analyses. It was discovered in 2002 that studies linking deaths to very fine particulate matter (such as diesel exhaust) were biased because of a default setting in a computer program.[15] The correction resulted in a revision of the estimate from a 0.41 per cent rise in mortality per 10 $\mu g/m^3$ of fine particles to a 0.27 per cent increase (Figure 2.3). The consequence was that transport pollution systems were safer than was thought originally. While this was good from a human health perspective, it imposed

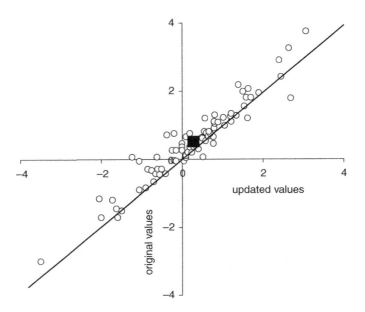

FIGURE 2.3 Bias in air pollution data resulting from a programming error.[16] The vertical distance of the circles from the diagonal line shows how much the estimated death rate was wrong for each of 90 cities (not all 90 are shown here). The black square shows the location of the pooled estimates (the updated estimate was 0.27 per cent per 10 mg/m^3 of PM_{10}, and the original was 0.41 per cent). PM10 are particles with a diameter of 10 micrometres or less. Source: adapted from Kaiser (2002).

significant, potentially unnecessary, costs on the transport industry to reduce pollution.

Natural variation and lack of knowledge are distinguished by whether collecting additional information reduces them. Collecting more and better data usually can reduce uncertainty arising from lack of knowledge. Natural variation is better understood and more reliably estimated, but it is not reduced by collecting additional data.

When there is an imperative to proceed with some course of action, but there are insufficient data to evaluate the consequences of doing so, the judgement of an expert may be used in place of data (the impetus for this book!). In all such assessments there are many elements of uncertainty.

The standard way of dealing with this type of uncertainty is to assign a degree of belief, in the form of a subjective probability, as introduced at the start of this chapter. For instance, an expert might assign a probability of 90 per cent to the event 'there will be an algal bloom in the lake this month'. This estimate might be based partly on frequency data. An expert's estimate will be uncertain but it should coincide with data if they are available. We will return to the idea of subjective probabilities below.

LINGUISTIC UNCERTAINTY

Linguistic uncertainty arises because language is not exact. For example 'it's raining' may apply when it is pouring or when a few drops sprinkle down.[17] The need for precision depends on context. It is not practical to subdivide meaning to cope with all circumstances. We can't have a different word for all degrees of rain intensity. Language needs to be compact. Generality is necessary for communication.

However, the trade-off is that linguistic uncertainties arise regularly in a variety of ways. Experts often communicate in language, rather than with numbers or formulae. Uncertainty may arise in vague, ambiguous, or underspecified expressions, and when context is not provided.

Experts are sometimes surprised to learn that unacknowledged linguistic uncertainty may affect scientific assessments. The following is a quote from a review of a paper that I wrote with colleagues on linguistic uncertainty in risk analysis: '*Discussing how to reduce linguistic uncertainty in a risk analysis is akin to telling a writer to avoid incomplete sentences and minimise the number of misspelled words. A professional already knows this and would be insulted if someone told him.*' Yet, we'll see below that it is easy to find examples in many scientific papers of instances where linguistic uncertainty can lead to qualitatively different interpretations of the results.

Vagueness arises because language permits borderline cases. Algae are always present in fresh water. At what point does an algal population become an 'algal bloom'? In practical terms, a bloom occurs when the density of algae is such that water appears green (or red), smells are emitted, oxygen is depleted, water becomes toxic, and fish die. The bloom is defined in terms of its consequences.

The term is still vague because it doesn't delineate, for example, between slight and severe algal blooms. It doesn't tell us what it means for the water to become toxic, or for emissions to become too smelly. A spurt of algal growth that turns the water slightly green may not count as a bloom to a fishing fleet if it has no impact on fish stocks. The vagueness of the term 'algal bloom' ensures that there is no straightforward answer to the question of how many algal blooms occur in a lake in a year.

A common strategy for eliminating vagueness is to replace the intuitive meaning with a sharp, technical boundary. For example, one operational definition of an algal bloom is one where the number of cells exceeds 5,000 per millilitre (ml) (usually in a single surface sample). While this definition is clear, it opens the door to sense-less decision-making.[18] Assume, for example, that this determines whether people are permitted to swim at a popular lake. At 4,999 cells per ml we say, 'jump in, the water's fine'. At 5,000 cells per ml, we tell everyone to go home. We open the weirs and flush the contaminating algae.

In most real circumstances, large effects are less likely, smaller ones are more likely. There is a continuum between them. As Figure 2.4 shows, we can't talk precisely about earthquakes or oil spills. Mostly these events are small, but there is a long tail of low-probability, high-consequence events. Decision-makers should be made aware of the full distribution of potential events, and the continuum of trade-offs of costs and benefits at each level.

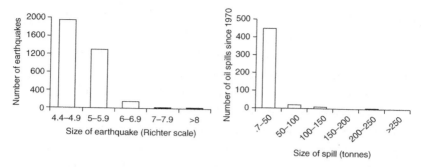

FIGURE 2.4 Many events generate a continuous range of outcomes. Events of the greatest magnitude typically occur with lower probability. The left-hand panel shows the annual frequency of earthquakes globally (the category 5–5.9 has a maximum of 13,000; smaller earthquakes are more numerous still).[19] The right-hand panel shows the frequency of oil spills from ocean-going tankers.[20] Sources: www.earthquake.usgs.gov and www.itopf.co.uk.

Context dependence arises from a failure to specify the context in which something is to be understood. For example, suppose an expert says an oil spill is 'small'. If the context is not specified, we are left wondering whether the oil spill is small for an oil container or a dinghy, small for a port or the open ocean. The International Federation of Oil Tanker Owners defines a large spill as one releasing more than 700 tonnes of oil.[21] A spill of half that size in your backyard would not be a small event. The way to deal with context dependence is to specify context.

Note that 'small' is also vague, but that vagueness and context-dependence are separate issues. Vagueness persists after the context has been fixed. That is, even after we are told the context – 'small-for-a-cargo-vessel-in-the-ocean', for example – there are still borderline cases. Borderline cases illustrate the concept of vagueness because it is unclear to which category something belongs. When does 'small' become 'large'? We can impose thresholds to address vagueness, but it is arbitrary to distinguish a 'small' 699-tonne spill from a 'large' 701-tonne spill, just as it is arbitrary to let people swim at 4,999 algal cells per ml and send them home at 5,000 cells per ml.

Decision-makers set thresholds that trade off the costs, for instance, of sending people home unnecessarily, against the costs of allowing them to swim and maybe become sick. It is best to make such trade-offs explicit, although often they are not.

Ambiguity is a form of linguistic uncertainty arising from the fact that a word can have more than one meaning and it is not clear which meaning is intended. It becomes problematic when experts are unaware that someone is using a meaning other than theirs.

I noted earlier that when Sherman Kent observed people in an intelligence agency using words for probabilities, the meanings for the term 'serious possibility' ranged from about 20 per cent to about 80 per cent. These differences were not apparent to the analysts or the decision-makers in the agency at the time. Kent then went about creating numerical scales that could be tied to words describing probabilities. These came to be known as 'Words of Estimative Probability'. I describe these shortly in more detail.

Underspecificity is yet another form of linguistic uncertainty that occurs when there is unwanted generality. For example, a weather forecast may state that there is a 70 per cent chance of rain.

Possible interpretations are:

- rain during 70 per cent of the day, so that if you emerge from a building at ten random moments, you will get wet on seven occasions (time);
- rain over 70 per cent of the area, so that if you ask ten people to stand at random locations outside for the day, seven of them will get wet (area);
- 70 per cent chance of at least some rain at a particular point, so that if you ask someone to stand by the weather station on ten days like this one, they will get wet on seven such days (days).

Psychologist Gerd Gigerenzer and his colleagues surveyed people's understanding of this question in several cities, asking what they thought it meant when a forecaster said that there is a 70 per cent chance of rain.[22] These were their results (Figure 2.5).

Typically, weather forecasters assume the latter (days), although it is rarely stated and may not be understood. People in New York mostly took the interpretation that was consistent

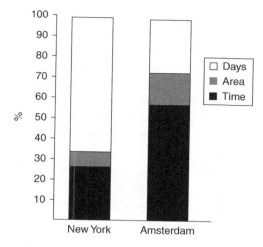

FIGURE 2.5 Proportions of the populations of New York and Amsterdam who believe that the statement 'a 70 per cent chance of rain' implies that it will rain for 70 per cent of the time during the day (time), that rain will fall over 70 per cent of the area (area), and that it will rain on seven out ten days such as this (days).
Source: adapted from Gigerenzer et al. (2005).[23]

with the forecasters. People in Amsterdam mostly didn't. In most instances, the statement 'there is a 70 per cent chance of rain' is sufficient to make a decision about how to dress, but it may be underspecific depending on a person's sensitivity to the outcome. Farmers, for instance, may prefer to have information reported using the second definition. The best we can do is to provide the information behind such statements.

WHAT IS A GOOD ESTIMATE?

Expert estimates can be wrong in many ways. So, what is a 'good' estimate? To answer this question for estimates of quantities on a continuous scale, it's helpful to break down the quality of an expert's judgement into four parts, some of which I touched on earlier.

1. *Accuracy* measures how close an expert's quantitative estimate is to the truth. Accuracy can be measured by the difference between an expert's

estimate and the correct answer. Over several questions, it may be the average difference.

2. *Bias* measures the tendency of an expert to deviate consistently from the truth in a single direction, to be either too high or too low. Bias can only be measured over the answers to several questions.

3. *Calibration* is the frequency with which uncertainty intervals enclose the truth, compared to the frequency with which the expert expects them to.[24] Calibration can be measured by counting, over several questions, the frequency with which the expert's intervals enclose the truth.

4. *Reliability* is a property of an expert rather than an individual judgement. It is the degree to which an expert's estimates are repeatable and stable. Reliability can be measured by how much an expert's accuracy, bias and calibration vary between problems.[25]

This list is incomplete but it's a useful starting point. Think about the answer to a question as a target on a number line (i.e. the 'fact' in Figure 2.6). Each arrow is an expert's best estimate of the fact. Each arrow should be accompanied by an interval that reflects the expert's uncertainty (not shown on the next diagram). Sets of arrows represent a group of experts estimating a single fact. Good estimates are accurate and well calibrated. A good judge is accurate, unbiased, well calibrated and reliable.

No expert can estimate all facts exactly because circumstances are unique, measurements are imprecise, and some processes are inherently unpredictable. So, how good is good enough?

The costs of inaccuracy, bias and poor calibration depend on the problem at hand. It may cost a lot if we trade oil futures and underestimate the future price of oil by 1 per cent. Alternatively, we may not care very much if we underestimate the number of people who visit a National Park by 50 per cent, if the site is well prepared.[26]

If we know that our expert is well calibrated, and she estimates a fact and a region of confidence around it, we will be able to develop robust plans to buffer us against uncertainty. For instance, we may ask an expert to estimate the number of cases of a disease that will arise in a population over the next 12 months. If her response is that

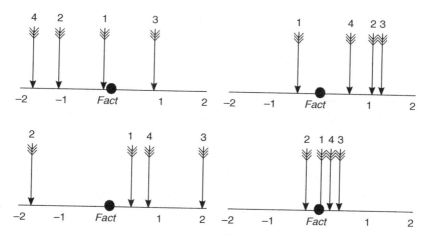

FIGURE 2.6 Expert 1 provided the most reliable estimates of these four facts (over all four questions, she appears to be unbiased and relatively accurate). Expert 3, in contrast, was biased and inaccurate. That is, she overestimated all four quantities and was relatively far from the truth.

she is 90 per cent sure there will be no more than 500 cases, we may budget for this number of treatments, knowing that in 9 years out of 10, the number of cases will be less than 500.

If an expert is routinely close to the truth but she provides very wide margins of confidence, her judgements are accurate but uninformative. If an expert provides narrow bounds but is routinely far from the truth, the judgements are misleading. If, however, the expert is routinely both close to the truth and confident, she is valuable.

In some circumstances, we ask experts to predict the outcomes of events, so that each question implies a yes/no answer. For questions with binary outcomes it's wise to allow the expert to specify how likely it is that the event will occur.

Suppose we put the question in the form 'will this event occur?' If the expert is absolutely sure it will happen he will respond 'yes', saying the probability is 100 per cent. If the outcome seems equivalent to the toss of a coin, he may say that the probability is 50 per cent. If he is reasonably sure that the event will not occur, he may say that the probability is 10 per cent. We can use this percentage judgement together with the outcome, once it occurs, to measure the accuracy of the expert's assessment.[27] Note that this is a bit different to the way we measure accuracy for judgements of simple quantities, but the principle of measuring the distance from the true value (or outcome) is the same.

It is more difficult to estimate the 'accuracy', or appropriateness, of expert advice on questions about a preferred option, portfolio or course of action.[28] Generally, there is no standard against which to judge individual recommendations. Something that seems good for one party may be less so for another. However, in cases where values are shared (for example, most people value human health), an expert's advice will seem good if it leads us to a course of action that is satisfactory. If the action leads to disaster, we feel chagrined. We can learn about an expert's performance only by observing the outcomes of many such judgements.

Life is a gamble. The best we can expect is that the expert will understand our personal goals and context. The expert may provide a course of action that keeps us relatively safe from harm, and that maximises our chances of a better-than-expected outcome.

The abilities of experts can be measured if we have relevant questions to which *we* know the answers, but the experts do not. That is, we can validate experts with independent data. We can obtain such data from hypothetical models, retrospective studies, or monitoring. As long as the experts haven't seen the data they can be tested against it. We will explore this idea in more detail later, but it forms the core of the approach promulgated by Roger Cooke and his colleagues.

The frailties discussed so far might prompt the question as to whether expert estimates are good enough to use at all. I explore these weaknesses in more detail in Chapter 3.

ALL JUDGEMENTS ARE UNCERTAIN

The categories for uncertainty presented here are not the only ones possible. Not all uncertainty can be neatly classified into one, and only one, category. Other classifications of uncertainty have been devised with different emphases.[29]

Methods for treating different kinds of uncertainty differ. For instance, none of the methods used for dealing with linguistic uncertainty are probabilistic, while many strategies for treating natural variation are. We will return to the question of how to deal with different kinds of uncertainty, and the role it plays in expert judgement, in the following chapters.

All estimates and predictions are uncertain. There is a tendency to think that a system has failed when there is an unwanted and unanticipated outcome. Sometimes, an intelligence agency does not identify a threat in time to prevent an attack. A mine manager may not identify a hazard before a worker is injured. Or a quarantine officer may not take an action that otherwise would have prevented a pest or disease entering a country. When these events are visible or newsworthy, organisations and the public may embark on a blame game.[30] We want someone to be responsible for the event in question.

While we can learn from such failures, there is no such thing as zero risk. When we say there's a 95 per cent chance that we will detect all cases of disease, for instance, we are also saying that 5 times in 100, we will not detect cases of a disease. The most we can hope for is that the experts know that this kind of event may occur, and that their estimate of the frequency of the event is in line with the actual frequency.

Whenever you need expert judgement, it is wise to keep in mind that the experts themselves may be unaware that different kinds of uncertainty may affect their judgements. They also may be unaware of the drivers that lead them to biased and inaccurate assessments, which is the topic of the next chapter.

3   What leads experts astray?

It is important to reiterate a point from the first chapter. This book is NOT about practical skills honed by repetition – such as plumbing, bridge building or surgery – nor is it about judgements related to such skill-based tasks. Rather, it deals with technical estimates and predictions of unknown quantities or future events made by people whose standing is defined by their qualifications, experience and status among their peers.

When we think of the kind of expert we'd like to consult for a prediction or estimate, we often think of someone middle-aged (or certainly not too young), with excellent training and qualifications, and ample relevant experience. We imagine a thoughtful and attentive person who is held in high esteem by their peers. Often, the property of 'being an expert' is taken to be self-evident.[1] It is someone whom everyone else agrees is an expert.

When governments and other institutions set up expert panels they look for many of the same attributes; they examine reputation, qualifications, track record, professional standing and experience.[2] Similarly, courts and statutory bodies accept expert opinion because they believe experts have specialised knowledge not available to all. In their view, it is obtained through training and experience. It is proven by track records of efficient and effective application.[3]

How should a manager or decision-maker decide which experts to consult? If we subscribe to the conventional definition of expertise, we just need a pool of qualified people. Literature reviews would be useful to define the expert pool because books and articles in scholarly journals reflect qualifications and experience. Frequently, experts suggest other experts who suggest others, and so on (termed 'snowballing'[4]). This approach assumes that experts are able to identify other similarly trained and experienced people who will provide reliable estimates of facts.[5]

In general, the strategies above are effective for finding a skill-based specialist. When the task is learned by training and repetition, when the outcomes are tied unambiguously to the person who performed them, and when we can examine a record of performance, then reputation and track record are a useful guide to performance.

Unfortunately, when making difficult judgements in unpredictable environments, these strategies for identifying the best judge may not be helpful. In many situations, you would do just as well to draw names out of a hat. The final chapters of this book outline fresh approaches that will help decision-makers to get the best out of experts, even when the tasks involve prediction and estimation under uncertainty. Before then, however, I will justify the claims that conventional expert judgements are frail and that status and experience are poor guides to performance among experts. We will also see that experts nevertheless can usually outperform untrained or 'lay' estimates, albeit by a lesser margin than we might hope.

STATUS AND STYLES OF REASONING

During the 1980s, Philip Tetlock began asking experts, conventionally defined, to predict the outcomes of geopolitical events. Over a 20-year study[6] he canvassed hundreds of government officials, journalists, academics and others considered to be experts in geopolitics. He asked them to make many predictions. He then waited and documented what actually happened.

He made two remarkable findings. First, the experts were only slightly more accurate than chance. For example, almost as many experts as not thought that the Soviet Communist Party would stay in power until at least 1993, that the Economic and Monetary Union in Europe would collapse by 1996, and that George Bush Senior would be re-elected in 1992. Second, while some people were much better than others at making predictions, the people who were best at predicting outcomes were not necessarily more experienced or more highly trained. In fact, the only thing that explained some of a person's predictive abilities was their 'cognitive style'. People who were good at making predictions typically drew information from a number of sources, thought about different explanations and did not make judgements according to a single idea or theory.

Conventional attributes of experts were, at best, a weak guide to their abilities to predict. But can experts themselves distinguish reliable experts from unreliable ones? That is, do they know one another's abilities well enough to be able to recommend the right person?

Together with colleagues, I explored this by asking experts to rank how well they thought their peers would answer sets of relevant technical questions.[7] We called these 'peer assessments'. We also asked them to rank themselves. We called these 'self-assessments'.

Prior to assessing one another, participants who didn't know one another spent a minute describing their training, experience, publications, memberships and so on, the kinds of information a person would provide in court to support expert testimony. We repeated the experiment in six workshops involving different kinds of life scientist, including botanists, medical scientists, biosecurity specialists, frog biologists and weed scientists.

There were two interesting findings from this study. First, our belief about our own performance on matters of technical detail is very much in line with the beliefs that other people have about us. Figure 3.1 shows the scatter of points relating self-assessments to peer assessments. The dashed line is where the points would fall if the groups scored people exactly as they scored themselves. The scatter of points is quite close to the dashed line, indicating that self-assessments and peer assessments are similar. The overall correlation between self-assessments and peer assessments was 0.85.

This result says that people assess our abilities similarly to our assessment of our own abilities. These are deeply held, shared social beliefs about performance on matters of fact. It is interesting to note

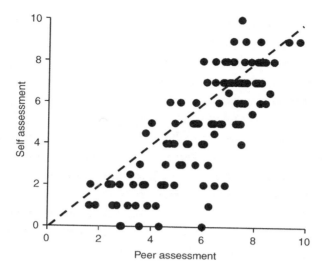

FIGURE 3.1 Expected performance on technical questions. 'Peer assessment' was the score out of 10 that people in workshops thought their peers would achieve on sets of technical questions from their domain.[8] 'Self assessment' was the score out of 10 that participants in the workshops thought they themselves would achieve on the same questions. Source: Burgman et al. (2011b).

that the assessments may be formed within a minute of the participants meeting one another.

The scores for peer assessment correlated positively with the conventional definitions of expertise discussed above, namely, age, experience, qualifications, seniority and publications. That is, we expect more experienced and better-credentialled people to provide more accurate answers to technical questions than less experienced people. Women, younger and less experienced people tended to rate themselves less highly.

Note that dots corresponding to a score below about 5 on the horizontal axis tend to fall below the dashed line. More dots above a score of about 5 fall above the dashed line. This says that people who rate themselves highly tend to rate themselves higher than does the group. Put another way, older, better-credentialled and more senior people tend to show less humility.

So should we expect these more self-assured people to also perform better? Volcanologist Willy Aspinall examined the judgements of geophysicists, remarking, '[a]s is often the case, several experts were very sure of their judgement and provided very narrow uncertainty ranges. But the more cautious experts with longer time estimates and wider uncertainty ranges did better on the [test] questions ... Their views would probably have been poorly represented if the decision had rested on a group discussion in which charismatic, confident personalities might carry the day. Selfconfidence is not a good predictor of expert performance...'[9]

Radiologist Michael Potchen[10] found a similar phenomenon when he examined the accuracy of diagnoses by 95 certified radiologists. The top 20 had an average accuracy rate of 95 per cent. The bottom 20 had an accuracy rate of 75 per cent. Yet, the bottom performers had more confidence in the accuracy of their diagnoses than did the top performers.

So, how did the experts perform in our study? The six panels in Figure 3.2 show the results for the six workshops in which people answered sets of test questions relevant to them. Each panel shows the relationship between the peer assessment scores for each participant and the average errors they made in answering the questions. Values on the vertical axis closer to zero represent better performance.

If older, more experienced and better-regarded people made better estimates, we would expect their estimates to be closer to the truth. More lowly ranked people should have greater errors. Thus, we should see dots on the left-hand side of each panel that are generally higher (further from the x-axis) than are dots on the right-hand side of each panel. There are no such patterns.

Basically, there is no relationship between an expert's status, their own or their peers' expectations of their performance on questions of fact, and how they actually perform. This result replicates Meehl's observations that experience and the level of training achieved by medical clinicians seem to make little or no difference to their abilities to predict accurately,[12,13] and Cooke's observations

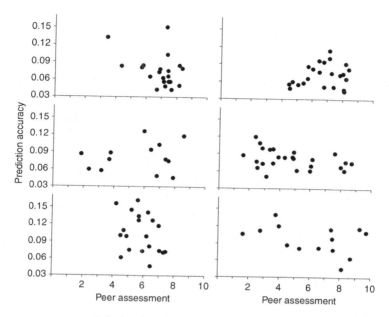

FIGURE 3.2 Relationships between peer expectations of performance on test questions and actual performance. The y-axis is the error in peoples' estimates.[11] Estimates were scaled by the range (max–min) of responses to each question. The figures for self-assessment versus prediction accuracy are qualitatively the same. There is no pattern. Source: Burgman et al. (2011b).

of the lack of a relationship between accuracy of estimates and peer status among engineers.[14]

It is important to remember that these people were all experts, to some extent. They were familiar with the jargon and the contexts of the questions. That is, they had enough experience or training to know what was being asked. They also had a chance to discuss the questions and clarify language or meaning before answering them.

These results tell us that we cannot expect an expert to know the limits of her own expertise. Nor can we expect her to know who, among her colleagues, will be accurate.

An expert's lack of self-awareness seems to be learned early. When college students were asked how well they think they did on a test, high-performing students estimated their outcomes accurately, if slightly modestly (Figure 3.3). Low-performing students have grossly inflated opinions about their abilities. Psychologist David Dunning concluded that, if people lack the ability to produce correct answers, they are also cursed with the inability to know whether their answers, or anyone else's, are right or wrong.[15,16]

The confidence that experts have in their own judgements is not entirely barren. If used carefully, it can be informative in some circumstances.[17] Consider the following situation: after a medical test, a doctor provides a worrying diagnosis. Despite the doctor's high confidence in her conclusion, you seek a second opinion. The second doctor's diagnosis is benign. But his level of confidence is lower than the first doctor's. Whose opinion should you believe? If the decision environment is 'kind' (in the above example, that means diagnostic error rates for the test are low and the prevalence of the disease in the population is not too rare), then you should accept the more confident judgement.[18] However, take care. If the decision environment is 'wicked' – for example, error rates are high – confidence can be misleading.

Figure 3.4 shows army doctors' subjective estimates of probabilities that patients have pneumonia. They were a poor predictor of the outcomes of more reliable diagnoses based on radiography. In another study, when nuclear experts were asked about the longevity

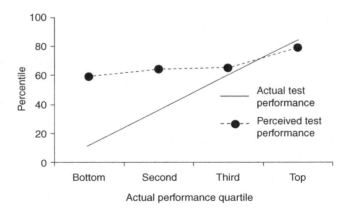

FIGURE 3.3 Differences between students' expectations of the outcomes of a test and their actual performances.
Source: adapted from Denning et al. (2003).[19]

of safety systems, they underestimated the lifetimes of long-lived components and overestimated the lifetime of short-lived components. Ed Capen, a petroleum engineer, anticipated these results when he said in 1976, '[e]very test we have performed points in the same direction ... The average smart, competent engineer is going to have a tough time coming up with reasonable probabilities...'.[20] Performances of experts in business, energy planning and military intelligence are similarly mixed and often unimpressive.[21]

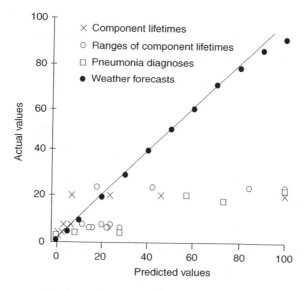

FIGURE 3.4 Expert predictions can be plotted against actual outcomes in calibration curves. Here, crosses are estimates by engineers of the mean lifetime of components in nuclear power systems, versus measured lifetimes. Open circles are estimates of the ranges for the mean lifetimes of the same components, versus measured ranges. Ranges are expressed as the maximum divided by the minimum. The components included pumps, valves and heat-exchange units.[22] The squares are army doctors' subjective probabilities that patients have pneumonia, versus more reliable diagnoses based on radiography.[23] Solid circles are meteorologists' predictions for the probability of rain on the following day, against the observed relative frequencies.[24] The diagonal line provides the line of correct estimation for all sets of observations. Values are scaled so that the maximum value in each set is 100.
Sources: Mosleh (1987) in Cooke (1991); Christense-Szalanski and Bushyhead (1981); and Murphy and Winkler (1977, 1984) in Plous (1993).

So why do we see such mixed performance in expert judgement? The striking thing about Figure 3.4 is how well the weather forecasters do. How can that be, when people routinely joke about inaccurate weather forecasts?

Different disciplines have evolved different ways of dealing with uncertainty. Most remain mired in the conventional, unwarranted belief in unaided, unstructured expert judgement, characterised by 'going with your gut'. Others admit uncertainty. They develop methods to provide instant personal feedback. They train, use models to assist prediction, and data to validate estimates. Meteorologists took this path. Consequently, they make better predictions. That is, unlike most scientific disciplines, they have turned the task of prediction into a skill.

I do not mean to imply that data-driven models give perfect forecasts. The world walked into the global financial crisis of 2007 with the help of quantitative models.[25] Rather, when it comes to estimating narrowly defined facts, we know we can do better than unaided subjective judgement. One of the strengths of meteorologists is that they know their own limits; they don't claim to make reliable predictions more than about five days in advance.

The performances of professional gamblers (Figure 3.5), weather forecasters and bridge players are *substantially* better than untrained or inexperienced people who attempt the same tasks.[26] Yet we don't usually associate these groups with good predictions.

ARE EXPERTS BETTER THAN NON-EXPERTS?

A person's formal training and technical knowledge are known as their 'substantive' expertise.[27] The knowledge of people with no formal training is known as 'lay' knowledge. When we ask questions of experts we expect their estimates of facts to be generally better than lay estimates, within the expert's area of expertise. Given the error-prone nature of expert estimates, is it worth consulting experts or should we just rely on our own estimates?

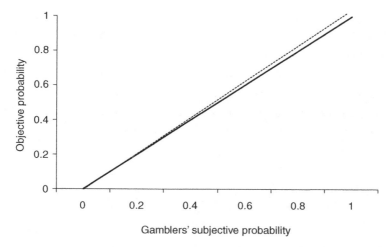

FIGURE 3.5 The relationship between gamblers' subjective probability estimates for the likelihood of winners in horse races (based on their actual bets; the dashed line) versus the objective probability of winning (the solid line). Their estimates are almost perfect. Source: adapted from Johnson and Bruce (2001).[28]

The answer is that, generally, experts make more accurate estimates than do non-experts, within their domain of expertise. In an influential study, Baruch Fischhoff and his colleagues[29] asked experts in insurance risk and lay people to estimate the number of annual fatalities from 25 technologies and activities. They compared the estimates to independent technical data.

The results are shown in Figure 3.6. Each point represents the average responses of the participants. The dashed lines are the straight lines that best fit the points. If people's estimates were reliable, the black dots and the dashed line would fall close to the solid diagonal lines. Unfortunately, they don't. The estimates of the risk of dying as a consequence of having a gun at home are highlighted. Lay people underestimated the risk by roughly a hundredfold, and experts by tenfold.

On the whole, the experts' estimates (indicated by the dots and the dashed line) were closer to the actual data (indicated by the diagonal solid lines) than were lay estimates. But they were not as close as one might expect. Both groups substantially underestimated the risks of high-probability events, and overestimated the risks of low-probability events. In some cases, lay people misjudged by two or three orders of magnitude. This experiment was repeated[30] using insurance underwriters (experts) and students (novices). While experts were better at ranking potentially lethal events, the differences between students and experts were small and their biases were similar.

In another experiment, I asked 14 biosecurity experts ten questions about disease rates, the timing of incursions of pests, the contamination levels in traded goods and related matters. A group of 15 people of equivalent ages and levels of education, but with no particular exposure to biosecurity issues, were given the same questions. The nonexperts performed worse (Figure 3.7).

Most (but not all) results from other disciplines tell a similar story. Psychologist Austin Grigg asked three groups (expert clinicians, graduate student trainees in psychology and untrained people) to listen to ten-minute interviews with three clients. He then asked them to predict how each client would fill out three different personality tests. There was no notable difference in accuracy between fully trained clinicians and trainees, but both groups did better than the untrained people. Thus, a small amount of expertise was useful.[31] Interestingly, physical scientists did as well as the clinicians and trainees.[32]

In 1976, George Wise summarised 1,556 social, technological, economic, and political predictions published in the United States between 1890 and 1940 and compared them with the actual outcomes. He looked at the qualifications and expert status of the people making the predictions. People with relevant experience did slightly better than inexperienced people. Within any field, one expert was as good as another.[33] This result was mirrored by the detailed examinations of expert political judgement made later by psychologist and political scientist Philip Tetlock.[34] He found that those with a modest

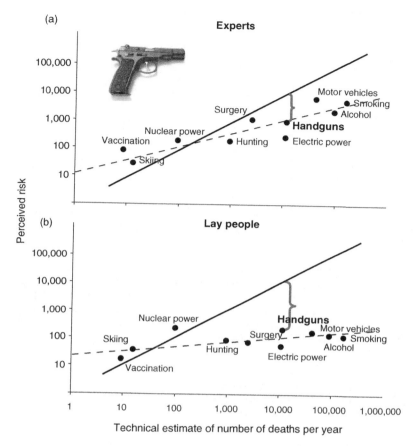

FIGURE 3.6 Averages of risk estimates made by (a) 15 experts and (b) 40 lay people plotted against the best technical estimates of annual fatalities for a range of technologies and activities. The experts included geographers, biochemists and hazardous-material regulators. The lay people were from the US League of Women Voters. The dashed lines are the straight lines that best fit the points. Both groups were biased. The experts' risk judgements were more closely associated with annual fatality rates than were lay judgements. The solid diagonal lines give the correct assessments.

Source: Fischhoff, Slovic and Lichtenstein (1982).

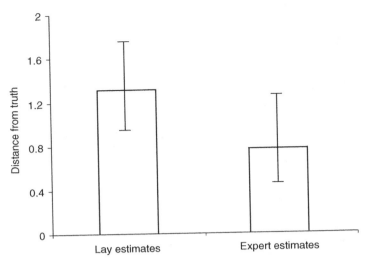

FIGURE 3.7 Accuracy of ten technical estimates by 14 experts (biosecurity professionals) and 15 lay people (masters students with backgrounds in engineering, commerce, science and other disciplines, but with no experience in biosecurity). The figure shows the group average response and 95 per cent confidence intervals. Estimates were scaled by the range (max–min) of responses to each question. Error bars are 95 per cent confidence intervals.

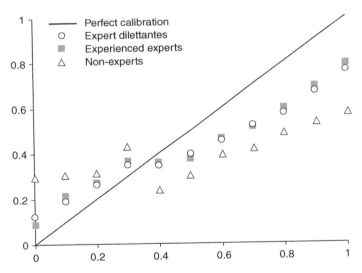

FIGURE 3.8 Comparisons between expert, dilettante and novice predictions for the outcomes of geopolitical events.[35] See equivalent examples for cardiologists,[36] nurses[37] and money managers.[38]

amount of training (expert dilettantes) performed as well as experienced experts (Figure 3.8). Additional experience did not improve a person's ability to predict.

The broad conclusion seems to be that experts (defined by the conventional criteria of training, status and experience) make better estimates and predictions than do untrained people, but not substantially better.[39]

This does not mean that lay knowledge is useless. Many people have a view that knowledge held by suitably qualified experts is an objectively defined 'truth', while knowledge held by lay people – usually stakeholders and the public – is fuzzy and oversimplified.[40] Such prejudices work in both directions. Another common misconception is that all lay knowledge is grounded in real-world, operational conditions. Many believe that it is concrete and sensitive to local realities while technical expertise is too theoretical to be useful.[41]

PSYCHOLOGICAL BIASES

In Chapter 1, I described how psychologist Daniel Kahneman was perplexed at his susceptibility to a bias that he called 'the illusion of validity'. He had sound evidence that his judgements were no better than random, yet he continued to believe them anyway. Subsequently, he and Amos Tversky conducted experiments on the ways in which people perceive and react to risks. Their results were strikingly counterintuitive and led to exciting generalisations. Among them, they found that people perceive change in relative, rather than absolute, terms and that, in general, people weigh losses more heavily than gains. They labelled this phenomenon 'loss aversion'.

Importantly, they found that experts and lay people are surprisingly sensitive to a host of psychological idiosyncrasies and biases.[42] Others took up the theme, and a significant research program around 'heuristics and biases' was established, which continues to discover quirks of human judgement and perception. I explore a few of the most important ones in detail below.

Decisions involve both facts and the desirability of what is to be gained or lost by the decision. Desirability is influenced by context and may change capriciously. Stockbroker Paul Bernstein recognised this when he stated, '*[f]ew people feel the same way about risk every day of their lives ... Investors as a group also alter their views about risk, causing significant changes in how they value the future streams of earnings that they expect stocks and long-term bonds to provide*'.[43]

Risk (or loss) aversion occurs when people prefer to have a smaller reward with greater certainty, than a larger reward with less certainty. This may be so, even when, on average, a person would do better to choose the high-risk, high-reward scenario. Risk aversion makes sense whenever the cost of losing a gamble would be unacceptable.

Economist Richard Thaler provided an example in which the prospect of loss influenced decisions more strongly than the prospect of gain.[44] He asked groups of people 'how much would you pay to eliminate a one-in-a-thousand chance of immediate death? And how much would you have to be paid to accept an additional one-in-a-thousand chance of immediate death?' It turned out that on average, people were prepared to pay only $200 to *eliminate* a one-in-a-thousand chance of immediate death, but they would have to be paid more than $50,000 to *accept* an additional one-in-a-thousand chance of immediate death.

In line with their convincing demonstrations of loss aversion, Kahneman and Tversky predicted that people would evaluate prospects with reference to the status quo. In one test of this idea, researchers presented improvements in the environment either as a gain compared to the current condition, or as the restoration to a previous condition before a loss was incurred. Improvement framed as returning a river system to an earlier, better state (loss recovery) was received much more favourably than was an identical program framed as improving the current status to some future, better state.[45]

The influences on judgement introduced here illustrate why context matters. For example, it is critical for an investment adviser

to know the personal circumstances, commitments and sensitivities of her client.[46] Without it, the adviser is unable to give sensible
advice. The adviser should also understand how a person's attitudes
may be strongly affected by how something is described, framed, or
presented.

Perceptual idiosyncrasies colour both expert and lay judgements.[47] It is important to remember that not everyone reacts like
this, just that the majority of people do.

Framing occurs when a change in presentation influences
behaviour surrounding the making of a choice, even when the objective characteristics are not changed.[48] Tversky and Kahneman[49]
described an experiment in which people chose a program to combat
a new disease expected to kill 600 people. The question was posed as
follows:

If program A is adopted, 200 people will be saved.
If program B is adopted, there is a one-third chance that 600 will be saved
and a two-thirds chance that no-one will be saved.

72 per cent of people preferred A to B.

They put the question differently to a separate set of people, as
follows:

If program C is adopted, 400 people will die.
If program D is adopted, there is a one-third chance that no-one will die,
and a two-thirds chance that 600 people will die.

22 per cent of people preferred C to D.

Of course, A and C are substantively the same, as are B and
D. Yet the preferences of most people were influenced by how
the question was framed. Tversky and Kahneman found the same
responses among undergraduate students, university faculty members and practicing physicians.

Another, separate study prompted Kahneman and Tversky to
coin the expression 'the law of small numbers', making an ironic
reference to the statistical law of large numbers.[50] It is also called
'insensitivity to sample size'. It means that most people – including

experienced scientists – draw inferences from data, especially from data they have collected themselves, that can only be justified with much larger samples.

For example, at a scientific meeting, I saw a fully credentialled research scientist document the behaviour of the release of a captive wombat. He described the path taken by this animal collected from a radio-tracking device. He then speculated about the behaviour of captive-bred wombats generally, following release into the wild. His results, based on the observations of a single wombat, could not sensibly be extrapolated at all.

The law of small numbers leads to estimates based on samples that are too small to generate reliable answers. People place undue confidence in early trends and over-interpret apparent patterns that turn out to be noise.

Yet another frailty is that of anchoring: the tendency to be influenced by a previously considered number. When asked to estimate a number, people tend to be drawn to the guesses made by others, or to an irrelevant number they have just seen. Biases arise when people are exposed to both plausible and implausible or irrelevant anchors.[51] This explains in part the law of small numbers: people anchor unreasonably on the results of small samples, especially if they are in line with results seen before.

Psychologist Paul Slovic and his colleagues[52] reported an anchoring study in which several thousand forensic expert psychologists and psychiatrists were shown case summaries of patients with mental disorders. The experts were divided randomly into two groups. The same case histories and questions were put to all the participants regarding the probability that a convicted person would re-offend after release. The two scales in Figure 3.9 were presented, one to each of the two groups of experts, as footnotes at the bottom of the first page. There was no requirement to use the scales. They were not referred to in the text of the summaries.

If you were one of the psychologists or psychiatrists who received the scale that ranged from 1 to 100 per cent, your estimate

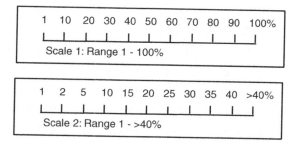

FIGURE 3.9 Participants were supplied randomly with one of two scales to assist them to make estimates of probabilities that violent criminals will re-offend. Source: adapted from Slovic et al. (2000).[53]

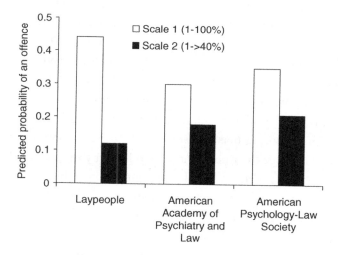

FIGURE 3.10 The influence of scale on experts' estimates. The members of the American Psychology-Law Society were given a tutorial on probability theory prior to their assessment.[54] In all cases, the sample sizes were at least several hundred individuals.
Sources: Slovic et al. (2000); and Gigerenzer (2002).

of the probability that the person would re-offend was roughly double that of the estimate you would have made had you received the scale that ranged from 1 to 40 per cent (Figure 3.10).

It is amazing that something so simple could have such a dramatic effect. It is an example of what Daniel Kahneman refers to as 'cognitive illusions'. People anchor easily on an irrelevant detail in the presentation. Thankfully, experts in this study were less strongly influenced than were lay people, but they were not immune to the effect, even though they were operating within the accepted limits of their professional expertise. The results were disquieting because expert psychiatrists and psychologists routinely make decisions on similar information that affect the lives of others in profound ways.

The tendency to anchor is pervasive and quite potent. In an early demonstration, Tversky and Kahneman asked participants to observe the spin of a numbered wheel. The wheel was predetermined to stop, arbitrarily, on either 10 or 65. Participants were then asked to guess the percentage of the United Nations that were African nations. The wheel had absolutely nothing to do with the question. However, people whose wheel stopped on 10 guessed 25 per cent on average, whereas people whose wheel stopped at 65 guessed 45 per cent on average. We are surprisingly sensitive to numerical cues and typically unaware of how important they are in shaping our judgements.

The anchoring bias is also related to the availability bias: the tendency to judge the importance of evidence by the ease with which examples are recalled.[55] People give greater weight to more vivid and memorable examples, giving them undue influence in subjective estimates. Recollections are influenced by the similarity of past experiences to the problem at hand. Catastrophic, newsworthy and recent events are more likely to be remembered, as are stark and unusual events.

Sometimes, more visceral processes drive our reactions. Generally, people are more afraid of being attacked by sharks whilst swimming than they are of travelling to the beach. However, you are more likely to die drowning or driving to the beach than to be attacked by a shark while you are there. More than 200 million people visit American beaches each year. Of those millions of beach-goers each year, about 36 are attacked by sharks (only a few of whom die), while more than 30,000 are rescued from surfing accidents.[56]

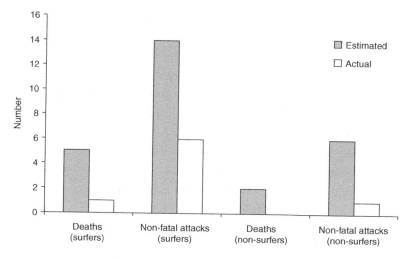

FIGURE 3.11 Estimated and documented attacks and fatalities on surfers and non-surfers by sharks between Cape Jervis and Goolwa, Australia, between 1955 and 2005.[57] Source: Lamb et al. (2005).

Even among relatively well-educated populations, such as those who live close to beaches and swim regularly, estimates of the frequency of attacks far outweigh the data. For instance, 113 residents living close to the coast between Cape Jervis and Goolwa in Australia were asked to estimate the number of fatal and non-fatal shark attacks that had occurred in their region in the last 50 years, among both surfers and non-surfers. There were substantial differences between the recorded and the estimated numbers (Figure 3.11).

Data aside, there is no getting around the visceral flight response elicited by the image in Figure 3.12. Even the word 'attack' is evocative, and implies physical harm. Yet 38 per cent of 'attacks' in New South Wales, Australia, between 1979 and 2009 did not involve any injuries, but were in fact sightings or close encounters.[58] But shark encounters are newsworthy, providing a vicarious thrill for mass media consumers. They are visible, memorable and frightening, and people overestimate the likelihood of attacks.

Visibility is one aspect of the availability bias that affects judgements, inflating perceptions of the importance of recent, newsworthy events. For example, part of the role of an emergency telephone operator is to screen calls and to eliminate 'obvious' hoaxes. Asking a few simple questions can do this. Most hoax callers hang up on being asked their name, address and the location from which they are calling.

False alarms are costly. Ambulances, fire fighters and police are expensive. False alarms divert scarce resources from other urgent cases. They are also commonplace. In some places, hoaxes make up as many as half of all emergency calls. The benefits of screening are that the response times to real emergencies are shortened and many lives are saved.

The cost is also considerable of failing to respond to urgent cases because they are thought to be hoaxes. Life-threatening emergencies may go unattended. This situation arose in Australia several years ago, with terrible consequences for an elderly woman. She was

FIGURE 3.12 Great white shark. Source: iStockphoto.com.

THE AGE
Thursday June 7, 2001
BREAKING NEWS www.theage.com.au

000 call woman left to die

By DARREN GOODSIR
and LES KENNEDY

A police phone operator dismissed a hoax 000 emergency call that an elderley woman had been left tied up and alive after being bashed and raped in her home. Her body was discovered by chance 10 days later.

Police last week apologised to Joy Golbey Alchin's family, saying 'the 70-year-old probably would have been found alive if they had responded to the call.

FIGURE 3.13 The consequences of deciding not to respond to an emergency call.
Source: *The Age*, Melbourne, Australia.[59]

attacked and tied to her bed. One of the attackers felt remorseful and later called the emergency number to report the incident anonymously. He was a young man, and when asked for his name and location, he hung up. The operator dismissed the call as a hoax, as are the vast majority of such calls. The elderly woman subsequently died. Had emergency services responded, she would have lived.

If the operator makes many such decisions and they are mostly right, then, on balance, this strategy will save lives by reducing response times, even if there is an occasional error. One might argue that the operator who incorrectly dismissed the call nevertheless made the right decision in the sense that more lives would be saved with this strategy than by assuming that all calls are serious.

However, this overlooks the emotional impact of the failure to respond to a real crisis. The elderly woman's death was highly visible (e.g. Figure 3.13) and led to substantial political pressure to respond to all emergency calls, no matter how implausible. Hoax calls result in delays that may result in deaths, but they are less apparent and therefore the reaction to them is muted.

Biases can also emerge through lack of independence resulting from shared conventional wisdom. If experts are assumed to be independent when they are not, overlap between their estimates will be taken as stronger evidence than is justified.[60] Engineer and risk analyst Vicki Bier suggested that if the technical base is narrow, or if people are selected by interpersonal relationships, they may represent a single school of thought or be influenced by the same data.[61] Even if there are small correlations between expert estimates, there may be little additional value in consulting more than a few experts.

CONDITIONAL JUDGEMENTS

Conditional judgements are estimates that depend on some special condition or property. For example, we may wish to estimate the chance that someone has a disease, given that they exhibit a relevant symptom. Most people find conditional judgements difficult, and experts are no exception.

Psychologist Gerd Gigerenzer[62] demonstrated that experts may be influenced by the way in which conditional information is worded. Consider the following example. The probability that a 40-year-old woman has breast cancer is about 1 per cent. If she has breast cancer, the chance that she tests positive in a mammogram is 90 per cent. If she does not have breast cancer, the chance that she tests positive is about 9 per cent. What are the chances that a woman who tests positive actually has breast cancer? It is very difficult for experts or anyone else to give the right answer (9 per cent) when information is presented like this.

Gigerenzer then restated the problem using natural frequencies instead of probabilities. Think of 100 women of age 40. One has breast cancer. She will probably test positive. Of the 99 who do not have breast cancer, nine will also test positive. How many of those

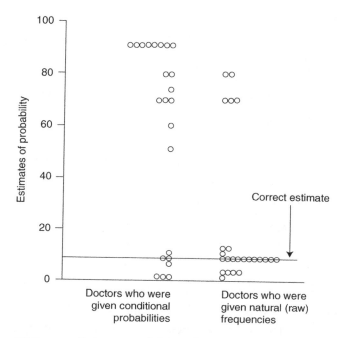

FIGURE 3.14 Estimates made by 48 physicians of the chance of breast cancer, given a positive screening mammogram. Half were given the information as conditional probabilities and half were given it as natural frequencies. When the doctors were given natural frequencies, their estimates clustered more closely around the correct value of 9 per cent. Source: adapted from Gigerenzer (2002).[63]

who test positive actually have breast cancer? The answer, one in ten, is now much easier to see. Figure 3.14 shows the guesses made by doctors who were given this information as percentages (conditional probabilities, left-hand side) and as natural frequencies (right-hand side). Those in the latter group were much more likely to interpret the positive test correctly.

One of the reasons why experts disagree is that they make use of different information. They make different assumptions about context and how cause and effect operate in a system. Decomposing problems and encouraging discussions to make assumptions visible can remove some of this uncertainty.

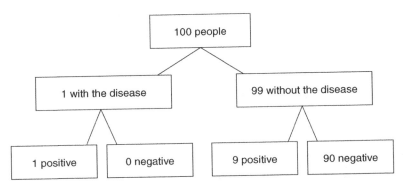

FIGURE 3.15 Considering the base rate of the disease and the failure rate of the test, what does it mean if your test comes back positive? Out of 100 women, 10 will test positive and 1 will have the disease.
Source: adapted from Gigerenzer (2002).[64]

The ease with which this problem can be solved using natural frequencies becomes even more apparent using a tree diagram (Figure 3.15). Despite such evidence, problems are rarely posed to experts in terms of natural frequencies. If they were, many mistakes could be avoided.

The problem that underlies the interpretation of conditional probabilities is allied to 'illusory certainty',[65] akin to Kahneman's illusion of validity. Our interpretation of the facts is distorted by the belief that scientific tests such as mammograms are infallible or highly reliable.[66] Lawyers suffer from the same flaw. It is termed the 'prosecutor's fallacy', and it means that lawyers and judges confuse the probability of an event with the probability that a particular person is guilty, given that the event occurred.[67]

OVERCONFIDENCE

I touched on overconfidence in Chapter 1, but it deserves to be treated in greater detail because unjustified optimism is such a pervasive feature of expert judgements. There are many striking examples. A few months before the meltdown of the Chernobyl nuclear reactor in Russia in 1986, and the release of substantial amounts of deadly radiation, the Ukrainian Minister of Power estimated the risk of a meltdown to be one in 10,000 years. As noted in Chapter 1, before the space shuttle *Challenger* exploded, NASA's official estimate of the risk of catastrophic failure was one in 100,000 launches,[68] yet space shuttles have a failure rate much closer to 1 in 100.[69] Both the *Challenger* and Chernobyl risk estimates were wildly overconfident. In many situations there is no positive relationship between an expert's confidence and their accuracy.[70]

There are some direct comparisons of expert engineers' estimates with actual outcomes, mostly collected by Roger Cooke and his colleagues. In Figure 3.16, for instance, experts estimated the probabilities of failure of seven components in a nuclear reactor safety system. Their judgements compared poorly to operating

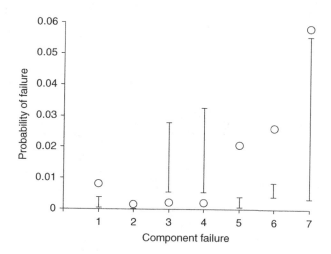

FIGURE 3.16 Ranges of expert estimates for probabilities of failure of seven nuclear reactor systems compared with actual outcomes (circles) at Oak Ridge in the USA.[71] The failures were (1–4, pressurised water reactor, 5–7, boiling water reactor) 1: small loss of coolant accident, 2: auxiliary feedwater system failure, 3: high-pressure injection failure, 4: long-term core-cooling failure, 5: small loss of coolant accident, 6: automatic depressurisation system demand, 7: high-pressure coolant injection. Source: adapted from Cooke (1991).

experience. None of the expert ranges captured the actual outcomes, reminiscent of the geotechnical expert assessments of embankment failure in the previous chapter. Whether they were 'close enough' depends on the implications of their errors for the safety of the nuclear power plant.

Results are similar for many other estimation tasks.[72] Most experts place greater confidence in their estimates and predictions than is warranted by data or experience.[73] Thus, experts have a region of overconfidence, a domain between the subset of facts they have learned or created and the subset they think they know (Figure 3.17).[74] It varies between experts and depends on how experts are questioned about their knowledge. But in general, experts lack humility about what they do not know,[75] which can make them dangerous.

Experts are most dangerous when the region of self-perceived but unjustified knowledge overlaps the region of perception by others. That is, the expert thinks they know something, *we* think they know something, but they don't. Once outside the narrow

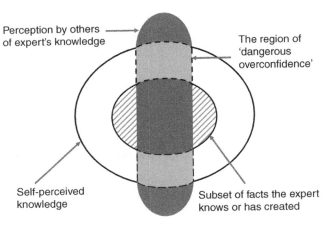

FIGURE 3.17 Expert knowledge and the region of overconfidence, situated between the subset of facts known by the expert and the subset they believe they know.
Source: adapted from Freudenburg (1999), and Ayyub (2001).[76]

domain of their core expertise, an expert is no more effective than anyone else.[77]

What's wrong with overconfidence? If we know it exists, can't we simply discount expert judgemental confidence appropriately? In short, yes, but we rarely do, expecting instead that experts will know the limits of their own expertise.

Overconfidence can lead risk-averse decision-makers to accept excessive risks – and therefore experience a higher frequency of poor outcomes than they are comfortable with. It can also lead risk-seeking decision-makers to decline tolerable risks and experience a lower frequency of good outcomes than they would prefer.[78] At the level of the individual, lawyers may be overconfident about the prospect of winning cases in which they are involved. They may, for instance, advise you to reject reasonable pre-trial offers.[79] Doctors may fail to consider alternative diagnoses and overlook 'defensive' treatments.[80]

If experts specify relatively wide uncertainty bounds, they admit lack of knowledge. The implication may be that the person specifying the widest bounds has the least knowledge, and their reputation may suffer.[81] Unjustified self-belief is fuelled by the self-serving nature of expert consultations. People want experts who are confident and credible. They are even more attractive if they are well-regarded members of professional societies. When Krinitzsky[82] completed his review of expert opinion in earthquake risk assessments in the 1990s, he commented that many experts are '*fee-hungry knaves, time servers, dodderers in their dotage...Yet, these and all sorts of other characters can pass inspections...*'. Experts may have specialist skills, but they easily stray outside their narrow domain and often are unaware when they cross the boundary.[83]

We should expect overconfidence. After all, overconfidence appears to serve individuals well. Exaggerated impressions of mastery and unrealistic optimism in one's own abilities are symptoms of good mental health.[84] These attributes associate with a person's abilities to work effectively and care about others. People with accurate self-awareness often are mildly clinically depressed or have low self-esteem. Confidence can increase ambition and morale, and is thus a useful attribute in work, sports, business and war. Self-belief enhances determination, persistence and the credibility of bluffing.[85]

MOTIVATIONAL BIASES

Motivational bias is the intentional or unintentional adjustment of an expert's objective estimates that results from the expert's values or their prospects for personal reward. Such biases are pervasive but, as we saw in Chapter 1, scientific experts often are unaware of them.

For example, a group of 20 researchers in climate change were asked in 1994 to estimate the effect of a 3°C global temperature change by 2090 on gross world product.[86] The participants included people researching scientific, economic, political, ecological and engineering aspects of climate change. Their responses are shown in Figure 3.18.

This figure is interesting because, although it is ostensibly asking experts to estimate matters of fact, several opinions are so divergent that intervals do not include the best estimates of other people. Other intervals fail to overlap at all.

I have shown this figure to many groups of scientists, students and the wider public. I ask them, can you guess the qualifications and training of the three experts who predicted the direst consequences, experts 15, 16 and 17? And can you guess the qualifications and training of the four experts who anticipated relatively benign outcomes, experts 1–4? In every instance, someone has said, unhesitatingly and correctly, the pessimists are ecologists and the optimists are economists.

How is it that we can predict someone's first qualification by his or her answers to a question about a fact? It is because we know that values and interests coincide with ostensibly factual estimates. It is not altogether surprising to us that estimates by economists would be up to 20 to 30 times lower than those of natural scientists.

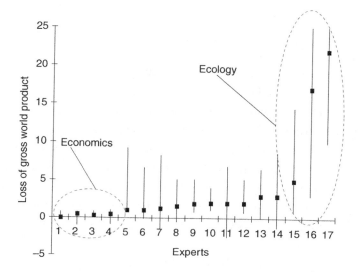

FIGURE 3.18 Best estimates and bounds for the loss of gross world product resulting from a doubling of atmospheric CO_2 by 2050, resulting in an increase in global mean temperatures of 3°C by 2090.[87] The intervals are 80 per cent uncertainty intervals (the 10th and 90th percentiles). Source: adapted from Nordhaus (1994), in Kammen and Hassenzahl (1999), Figure 4.3.

The entrenched opinions of experts within disciplines are apparent to almost everyone except, perhaps, to the people making the assessments.

At the very least, those making the assessments are often unaware of the *extent* of their bias. In one illustrative experiment, psychologists assigned buyer and seller roles to participants in an experiment, and asked them to assess the value of a firm.[88] Even with debiasing incentives for accuracy, sellers estimated the value of the firm to be almost twice as high as buyers. Although participants were aware that their roles may have influenced their appraisals, they seriously underestimated the size of their bias.[89]

Even well-intentioned people can provide biased assessments because it benefits them to do so. It can lead to overconfidence in predictions. For example, people in corporations acting as champions for a project are likely to emphasise potential benefits and understate costs. This is not due to malicious or cavalier attitudes in the proponents. It is a consequence of enthusiasm and ambition, positive attributes that breed optimism.

Similarly, technical experts may underestimate potential risks when their career prospects are tied to the development of the technology, even indirectly. For example, in the debate around the potential environmental risks associated with the release of genetically modified organisms, many ecologists argued for a strongly precautionary approach, comparing the risks involved with those of introducing an invasive species. Many molecular biologists argued that there was little or no risk based on the fact that genetic engineering strongly resembles long-standing and accepted practices of traditional breeding. The experience and values of the experts reflected the approach they took to the problem, their attitudes to uncertainty and the resulting conflicting empirical claims.[90]

Decision-makers themselves may introduce a bias by misinterpreting the information provided by experts, or by using it in models that have assumptions and functions that the expert would not agree with. This creates particular problems for the assessment of new technology risks. The few people with substantive knowledge are also likely to possess a motivational bias.

Other unwitting conflicts of interest arise. Gigerenzer[91] recorded a conversation in which a World Health Organization representative pointed out that roughly 44,000–98,000 people are killed in the United States each year by preventable medical errors, more than are killed by motor vehicles or AIDS. Safety systems such as those in commercial aviation that would be in the interests of the patient have not been set up in hospitals. Gigerenzer explained this anomaly by arguing that aviation safety is in the immediate interests of the pilot and crew, and the consequences of failure are highly visible and unambiguous.

Doctors and patients, on the other hand, sometimes have different, or even opposing, goals. For example, a physician may perform X-rays to detect fractures and to protect himself from potential accusations that may arise from overlooking a fracture. The patient may prefer to protect themselves from the harmful radiation to which they are exposed during an X-ray.[92]

One solution to these problems may be to penalise experts for errors that affect other stakeholders. But this sort of approach may be heavy-handed, especially where errors are caused by unintentional biases. Alternatively, the decision-maker or analyst may include a range of experts, where practicable. If each has a stake in the outcome, representing alternative scientific positions or different stakeholder groups, their biases may cancel each other out. We will explore approaches to combating motivational bias in the methods outlined in the chapters below.

CULTURE, GENDER AND INTUITION

Cultural differences contribute substantially to judgements, and different social groups react differently when confronted by the same issues. For example, gender and race are associated with apparent differences in attitudes to environmental risks and risk-taking behaviour in the United States.[93] Melissa Finucane and Paul Slovic asked groups of people to score hazards on a scale from one to five. Females and nonwhite males tended to rank things about the same. White males were, on average, more optimistic (Figure 3.19).

They called this the 'white-male effect'.[94] On closer inspection of the data, they discovered that the effect was driven by a subset of about 30 per cent of the white male population who were relatively well-educated, earned higher incomes and were politically conservative. They were substantially and consistently more optimistic about risks than most others in the population because they could afford to be so, and because they were less likely to bear the burden of the risk. The majority of the white male population (the other 70 per cent) was not particularly different from the other groups.

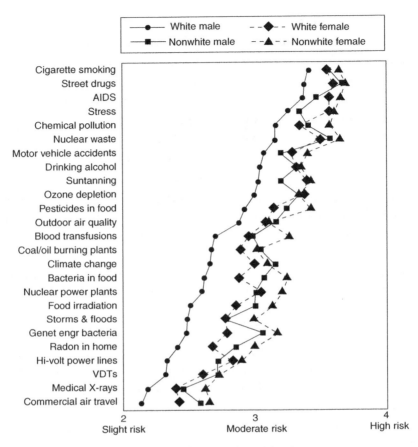

FIGURE 3.19 Mean risk-perception ratings for health hazards, differentiated by race and gender. Source: adapted from Slovic (1999).[95]

Males are relatively overconfident in many settings.[96] For example, in finance, male overconfidence is reflected in more excessive trading. Using trading records for over 35,000 households at a large discount brokerage firm, Barber and Odean (2001) found that the turnover rate of common stocks for men was almost 50 per cent higher than for women, and yet their annual returns performance was 0.93 percentage points lower.[97]

The acceptability of risk is a social quality. It is influenced by transparency and equitability.[98] Psychologists Wen-Qiang Bian and Robin Keller reported the attitudes of Americans and Chinese to risky situations.[99] One involved a choice either to take a 1 per cent chance of 100 people dying (and a 99 per cent chance that no-one dies), or to take one individual out of 100 (say, by a lottery) and sacrifice them to ensure that the other 99 remain safe. Both Chinese and Americans considered the former circumstance fairer, but most Chinese chose the latter course and most Americans chose the former. The Chinese population wanted to avoid a catastrophe. The authors speculated that the views reflected the greater importance attributed to collective actions in Chinese society.[100]

Judgement may be understood in terms of 'dual processing'. Daniel Kahneman calls it 'thinking fast and slow'.[101] 'Intuitive' thought processes are automatic, experimental, associated and reflexive. 'Analytic' thought processes are effortful, controlled, rational, systematic, rule-based and reflective. In general, intuitive (fast) and analytic (slow) processes are thought to act in parallel in most people. The two systems process information more or less independently, and may come to conflicting conclusions.[102]

Many people believe that 'gut' feelings, or intuitions, may provide important knowledge.[103] Intuition can be more accurate than analytic judgement, but only in very specific conditions, depending on the definition of 'intuition'.[104] Intuitions developed through extensive experience and consistent, immediate feedback can be effective in many professional domains.[105,106] For example, chess players, weather forecasters,[107] sports players, gamblers, intensive-care physicians and physicists solving textbook problems display accurate intuition because they receive instant feedback and because mistakes are visible and personal.[108] This kind of intuition accords with the phenomenon of skill-based performance that we discussed in Chapter 1. Another reason why good intuition may develop in these domains is that the solution is 'demonstrable'.[109] That is, the task can be demonstrated or proved, either through action or a verbal, mathematical, or logical system.

The ability to make relatively good predictions can also be explained, in part, by how people think. Psychologist Gerd Gigerenzer explains that people need rules of thumb, rough guidelines to help them navigate complicated situations, so that they can arrive at decisions that are 'good enough'.[110] However, when people think quickly they use different strategies. Some people like to try to explain everything with one basic theory or set of guidelines. Others try to draw information from as many sources as possible, encouraging those around them to contribute ideas. Following from Isaiah Berlin's original characterisation,[111] Philip Tetlock typified these latter people as 'foxes', as opposed to the more 'hedgehog'-like, single-theory types. We get into trouble when our fast-thinking systems rely on too few inputs and we fail to anticipate unique properties.

In a study of expert bush fire commanders predicting fire behaviour,[112] researchers showed 14 experienced commanders fire-detection points on a map and asked them to think aloud while predicting the final extent of the fires and deciding how the fires should be brought under control (Figure 3.20). Fires were selected from archival records, together with weather conditions and other information.

The spread of bush fires is determined by many factors, including temperature, wind speed, topography, the moisture content of vegetation and the amount and type of 'fuel'. In particular, wind usually drives the direction of spread. Uphill slopes and higher wind speeds accelerate the rate of spread. However, in light winds, fires can burn uphill against the direction of the wind.

The commanders made surprisingly accurate predictions for a 'typical' fire when the main predictor variables, slope and wind direction, indicated the same outcome. There was one 'anomalous' fire, which spread against the wind direction. Predictions were uniformly poor for the latter case.

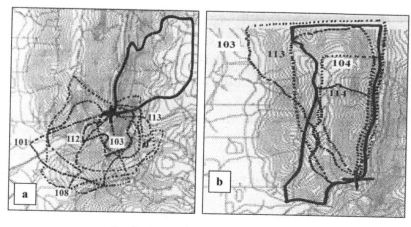

FIGURE 3.20 Prediction performance given the anomalous fire (panel a) and for a typical fire (panel b).[113] Fire-detection points are indicated by the bold cross. The actual final extents are enclosed by a solid border. Predicted final extents are shown by dashed outlines identified by participant number. Source: Lewandowsky and Kirsner (2000).

Analysis of their thinking suggested that the experts used a 'wind-first' heuristic, deriving fire direction from wind direction and then adjusting the rate (but not the direction) of spread by considering slope. This wind-first strategy was often successful, but failed systematically when wind and slope were in opposition and wind speed was low. Decision analyst Lynn Maguire noticed widespread use of such 'hazardous' mental short cuts in many other aspects of fire management.[114]

Intuitions tend to be inaccurate when feedback quality is low, circumstances are unique, or mistakes are not costly to those making the estimates. Delayed feedback, for example, makes it difficult for physicians and psychologists to learn about the accuracy of their diagnoses.[115] Where feedback is poor, experts are likely to have difficulty separating the influences of skill and chance, and tend to form superstitious beliefs.[116] Experts are unable to distinguish between skilled and unskilled intuitions, and will feel the same typically strong level of subjective confidence for each.[117]

THE HALF-LIFE OF FACTS

In 2002, physician Thierry Poynard and his colleagues published a remarkable review[118] assessing the frequency with which people writing about cirrhosis and hepatitis in scholarly medical journals made statements that, in retrospect, turned out to be obsolete or wrong. They documented scientific conclusions and recommendations published between 1945 and 1999. A total of 285 out of 474 conclusions in these papers were still considered to be true in 2000. A total of 91 observations (19 per cent) were obsolete and 98 observations (21 per cent) were wrong.

Figure 3.21 shows the proportion of studies whose conclusions remained true for periods following their first publication. An example of an obsolete conclusion is the efficacy of immunoglobulins for preventing infection by the hepatitis A virus. An effective vaccine is now available. An example of a false conclusion is the efficacy of corticosteroids for treating acute viral hepatitis; they don't help.

Poynard characterised this as the half-life of facts. On average, we should expect that about half the things we consider now to be

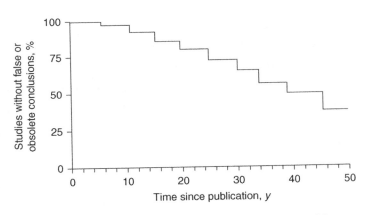

FIGURE 3.21 Decline in the proportion of studies without false or obsolete conclusions, from 100 per cent to below 50 per cent, as a function of the time since they were published.[119]
Data were from two journals, *Lancet* and *Gastroenterology*, published between 1945 and 1999, and assessed in 2000 (Poynard et al., 2002).

true will no longer be considered true in 50 years' time. Interestingly, Poynard found that the half-life of facts was not affected greatly by the quality of the methods in the studies. The findings from high-quality research were about as likely to turn out to be false or obsolete as were the findings from lower quality work.

It is possible that Poynard's work paints an overly optimistic picture of the longevity of facts in science more generally. He examined the discipline of medical science, which is relatively well organised and supported. He also selected studies only from two very well-respected, selective journals, *Lancet* and *Gastroenterology*. Facts in other disciplines may have shorter half-lives.

It is easy to think of other examples that once were facts. The earth is not flat. In fact, it is not quite round, either, but that's close enough for a general characterisation. The earth is not located at the centre of the solar system, although Galileo got into a lot of trouble with the Vatican for suggesting that it wasn't. Smoking is not generally a healthy activity, despite what doctors once advised.[120]

In 1992, an article appeared in the *Journal of the American Medical Association* showing that traditional review articles and textbooks often gave advice that was dangerously inconsistent with the evidence available at the time they were written.[121] Gaps between evidence and advice sometimes lasted more than a decade. Both effective and dangerous treatments were overlooked.

Another fascinating paper by another physician, John Ioannidis, underscored the fact that we should be wary of an expert's so-called facts, even when they are supported by published evidence. In 2005, Ioannidis made the startling claim that most published medical research findings are false.[122] Specifically, he blamed small sample sizes, small effect sizes, publication bias, and the pressure to publish, among other things.[123]

Ioannidis followed up his assertions by examining key clinical research studies in three major journals published between 1990 and 2003. He examined papers that were cited more than 1,000 times by subsequent papers.[124] One thousand citations is a lot – I dream of having such an influential paper. There were 49 such studies, of which 45 claimed that they had found an effective intervention or treatment.

He then compared the results of these highly cited articles with subsequent studies. Of the 45 highly cited studies that claimed an effective intervention, 7 (16 per cent) were contradicted by subsequent studies, 7 others (16 per cent) had found effects that were stronger than those of subsequent studies, 20 (44 per cent) were replicated, and 11 (24 per cent) remained largely unchallenged. For example, two large studies found that vitamin E was associated with a decreased risk of heart disease. However, a larger, better designed, randomised trial showed absolutely no beneficial effect of vitamin E. A small study of nine patients found that nitric oxide inhalation improved oxygenation in patients with respiratory distress. However, five randomised trials involving 535 patients failed to show any clinical benefit.

The unreliability of science is amplified in the 'discovery' phase of research. The effects of natural processes are inherently variable. Measurements are imprecise. The nature of discovery is that it is *'unfettered, haphazard, exploratory, opportunistic, selective, and highly subjectively interpreted'*.[125] During discovery, scientists are more likely to trip over a large effect size than a small one. Ioannidis suggested being cautious about interpreting the expected effects on interventions based on early studies, to the point of adjusting them or ignoring them altogether, at least until the studies have been replicated several times.

Ioannidis advised some general rules of thumb to anticipate these problems: research findings are less likely to be true if the number of studies is small, the effect sizes are small, experimental designs, definitions, outcomes, and analytical modes are diverse, the financial and other interests and prejudices in a scientific field are large, and the scientific field is 'hot' (with more scientific teams involved, competing for newsworthy results).

The lurching reversals of scientific truths are fodder for philosophers of science. Thomas Kuhn viewed scientific progress as a series of shifts from one dominant paradigm to the next, rather than the gradual acquisition of knowledge.[126] He argued that truth is defined by consensus in the scientific community rather than by objective criteria. Imre Lakatos noted that criticism may eventually refute things that had previously been considered to be truths, and the absence of criticism can allow conjectures to become regarded as truth.

Lakatos described how Euclid's geometry was proposed originally as a bold theory designed to challenge some of his contemporaries.[127] Only later were some of his ideas taken to be undeniably true and other more questionable 'axioms' were simply omitted from proof-analysis. The socialisation of Euclid's theories began with Aristotle, who branded one of Euclid's critics a 'quarrelsome crank'. It is interesting to note that, in Euclid's time, the word axiom meant a postulate put forward for testing, without being admitted as true. It is ironic that its meaning has been reversed so that, today, it means a starting point for reasoning, or a premise that can be accepted without proof.[128]

EXPERTS ARE HUMAN

Let's recap on the main points. Experts are susceptible to the normal range of human emotions and values. In addition, context may impose an inescapable bias on the pool of experts. Probabilities are difficult to estimate subjectively, especially when linked to hazardous outcomes, and particularly when they are conditional. Many factors colour estimates. I have introduced some of the most well-known factors in this chapter, including whether you're a privileged white male, whether you stand to lose or gain something from a decision, how terrible an outcome appears to be, or how visible it is. People's judgements are also coloured by fairness (people are less likely to tolerate a loss that they bear alone or with a subset of society, than they are to tolerate one shared more broadly), level of personal control (people tolerate higher risks of driving a car when they are behind the steering wheel than they will when riding in an aircraft, when someone else steers), whether a choice is voluntary (people will tolerate greater loss when they are given a choice than they will when the losses are imposed), and familiarity (people accept higher risks from familiar technologies).

We all share these psychological influences to varying degrees. Education and experience provide scant protection. Cognitive biases are heightened by politically charged and value-laden contexts such as when dealing with threatened species, or when organisational reputations are at stake (see details in Chapter 1). There may also be considerable pressure on experts to produce convincing projections, to diffuse social tension. They cannot occupy the independent, objective ground which politicians and policy-makers wish them to.

The extent of social and cognitive influences, taken together with the paucity of data in most circumstances, led Adams to conclude in his book about risk that *'risk may be viewed as culturally constructed, and context dependent. Risks can be changed, magnified, dramatised, or minimised, and so are open to social definition and construction. ... Risks are culturally constructed because sufficient facts are unavailable. Cases of genuine uncertainty are far more common than are cases in which risk is quantifiable. We must proceed in the absence of agreed facts'.*[129]

Arguments for the cultural construction of risk can be compelling. This perspective is reinforced by Poynard's observation that the 'truth' erodes over time. If they are right, technical views of expert judgement are misplaced. Credibility and trustworthiness may be more influential than data.

Routinely reliable estimates have only ever been demonstrated in people who make frequent, repeated, easily verified, unambiguous predictions so that they learn from feedback. The rest of this book is devoted to making the rest of us behave more like weather forecasters, bookmakers and bridge players, providing some help with the slippery issues that arise when these more typical, difficult conditions apply. People who are relatively successful in making technical estimates and predictions tend to work in narrow domains with enviable replication and relatively little ambiguity and social pressure. The rest of us are doomed to working in circumstances that hinder the kind of reliability afforded to these groups. But there is certainly room for improvement, even in complex, broad and highly uncertain domains.

WHO IS AN EXPERT?

There is no sharp distinction between expert and lay knowledge, just as there is no sharp distinction between data and expert judgement. What counts as relevant knowledge depends on the problem. It depends on the people involved and their social and practical circumstances.[130] Knowledge can be classified as 'expert' or 'lay' depending on its purpose, the interests it serves, and the manner in which it is generated.[131] We should acknowledge the normative and value-laden nature of scientific judgement, that political context influences scientific advice and may determine what comprises relevant, convincing evidence and that stakeholder participation, dialogue, and interaction weigh on important policy questions.

Social scientists take a relatively wide view of knowledge. For example, Collins and Evans[132] identified forms of expertise ranging from context-specific, local knowledge to specialist training. None of their categories depend exclusively on formal qualifications or professional memberships. The conventional requirements for suitable qualifications and professional standing may exclude people with relevant experience. My view is that anyone is a potential expert in the right context.

It should not only be experts (or well-informed lawyers) who can put critical questions to an expert. Anyone with a stake in the outcome should be able to question an expert's opinion. Decision-makers should avoid arbitrary, sharp, conventional delineations of expertise.

Instead they should develop processes to examine knowledge claims critically.[133]

Psychologists David Weiss and James Shanteau noted that many consultants who make economic and scientific forecasts do not have to perform well to maintain their status. Rather, their expert status is conferred by education and experience. While their credentials may be challenged, their work is not. They called this group 'privileged experts'. They are forgiven for mistakes and their errors are forgotten. Weiss and Shanteau speculate that this role persists because people believe, wrongly, that skilful people also make reliable predictions. Their solution is to develop a *'task-specific, performance-based, limited-term certification scheme'*. That is, they want to test experts, use some and disregard others. I outline recommendations for implementing such an approach in the last chapter of this book.

This chapter asks whether expert estimates and predictions are worth having. The answer is yes, but they are not as good as you might expect, and are not as good as the experts themselves believe them to be. Importantly, in many experiments, there is little appreciable difference between people who are conventionally thought of as being experts, and others with no formal qualifications or relatively little experience. That is, once a person has been exposed to a problem and understands the data, jargon and context, their estimates are as good as anyone else's.

Often we turn to experts to unload responsibility for a decision, or to advocate a position that coincides with our own. As a society, we uncritically accept this process due to the scientific authority and perceived objectivity of experts. If, however, the decision we confront depends on the veracity of facts – that is, if we genuinely care about the 'truth' – then we need to employ smarter strategies to engage with experts.

4   Dealing with individual experts

The experiences with experts and their frailties over the last 60 years have taught us an important lesson. People, including experts, have an overriding desire for a direct line to certainty. Because of this, we call on experts to make estimates outside the bounds of their expertise. The experts are willing to provide them. This chapter outlines some first steps towards shedding our naïve views of expertise, and embracing the philosophy that expert judgement should be treated with the same care and constructive scepticism that we afford to data.

Unreliable opinions can be uncovered, excluded or adjusted when they are tested against independent information. Strategies for doing so should be decided before the expert advice is received. If not, outcomes may be contaminated by the prejudices and context of the analyst or group that has control over the decision. Note that, when I refer to the 'analyst', I am referring to the person responsible for extracting and combining information from experts. They may be the facilitator and/or the decision-maker.

Post-hoc adjustment of expert estimates is one possibility for mitigating biases, for example, when we know that the biases are systematic because we have compared previous estimates against facts. But what else can be done to improve the quality of estimates?

There are several options. We can widen the set of experiences and skills of the pool of people we consult. We can test the knowledge of potential contributors and train experts to make good estimates. Finally, we can use procedures that minimise biases, and encourage honest opinions and critical examination of evidence. This chapter outlines some simple prescriptions for dealing with an individual expert to estimate a precise fact or predict the outcome of an event. The following chapter deals with group dynamics.

STRUCTURED QUESTIONS FOR QUANTITIES

My colleagues and I recommend a structured procedure for questioning experts about quantities[1] that uses four questions, termed a four-point format (Figure 4.1).[2] We use three questions, termed a three-point format, to elicit probabilities, which is outlined in the next section. In both cases, we elicit an interval to capture uncertainty.[3]

The first step in adopting one of these formats is to draft a question that seeks a precise, unambiguous quantity. It should pass what psychologist Ruth Beyth-Marom calls the 'clairvoyance' test:[4] can a question be stated sufficiently clearly that a clairvoyant, relying solely on facts, would be able to say whether the statement is true or false? It is usually necessary to test question formats to reduce linguistic uncertainty.

Once the question is finalised, the four-point format can be provided to the experts using the sequence of questions shown in Figure 4.1. This approach draws on research from psychology on the effects of question formats,[5] mitigating much of the overconfidence typically observed in expert estimates.[6]

In the four-point approach, we intentionally ask for the bounds before asking for the best estimate, to make people think about extreme values,[7] and to prevent them from anchoring on their best estimate. Usually, we preface the questions with a statement such as, for the first question: *Think about all of the data and reasons why the value may be small. With these in mind, realistically, what do you think is the lowest plausible bound?* And for the second question: *Think about all of the data and reasons why the value may be large. With these in mind, realistically, what do you think is the highest plausible bound?*

Note that the bounds don't have to be symmetrical around the best estimate. That is, a person may be more confident about an upper bound than they are about a lower bound, or vice versa.[8]

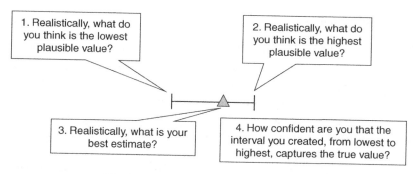

FIGURE 4.1 The four-point format for questions about quantities.

FIGURE 4.2 Estimating the number of jellybeans in a jar.

So, give it a try. Consider the picture of jellybeans in a jar (Figure 4.2). It's a jar of jellybeans. *What is your expert estimate of the number of beans in this particular jar, including the ones that have spilled in front?*

Use the recommended question format.

- First, consider all the things that might lead you to conclude a low number. For example, think about the curvature of the jar, and so on. With these things in mind, realistically, what do you think is the smallest plausible number? Take a moment to write it down, or commit it unchangeably to memory.
- Second, consider all the things that might lead you to conclude a high number. For example, the way the beans are packed. With these things in mind, realistically, what do you think is the largest plausible number? Take a moment to write it down, or commit it unchangeably to memory.
- Third, thinking of all the things that contribute to your estimate, on balance, what is your best guess? (You'll find the answer in the endnotes.[9])
- Finally, how sure are you that the true value lies between the lower and upper bounds you have just created? Provide a number between 50 per cent and 100 per cent.

The interval between your low number and your high number includes the estimates that you think are credible. To complete the picture, we would rescale your interval so that it is equivalent to a reasonably high level of confidence; say, a 90 per cent interval. Thus, if you provided an interval of 60 per cent, we would make it wider, so that it encompassed 90 per cent of your beliefs.[10] We do this to compare and combine intervals from individual experts. We also do it because intervals with really low confidence are (usually) not very informative.[11] For example, if you are 50 per cent sure that your interval encloses the true value, then you think the true value is just as likely to be outside your interval as inside it.

You should interpret your confidence estimate as though it were a frequency of repeated events. Your estimates over many questions should calibrate with the prescribed confidence. For example, if you provided ten intervals in response to ten questions and specified 50 per cent certainty for each interval, then the true value should fall within your intervals, five times out of ten.

If your interval for the jellybean question does not include the truth, don't be concerned. Many people's intervals don't. In fact, when we ask this question and rescale people's intervals so that they are all 90 per cent credible intervals, roughly five out of ten intervals enclose the right answer, when it should be nine out of ten. If we ask people more simply to provide an interval such that they are 90 per cent sure it will enclose the truth, roughly four of the intervals do so.[12] Thus, while the four-point question format reduces overconfidence, it does not eliminate it altogether.

People are routinely overconfident when answering this question, and most other questions for that matter. The jellybean question is one for which you are an expert. You understand the concept. The question is unambiguous. You are familiar with jellybeans and glass jars. You know enough about the topic to know what's being asked. The questions we put to technical and scientific experts are typically much harder than this.

Unfortunately, as questions become harder, overconfidence increases.

Let's try another question. *How far is it between Los Angeles and San Francisco?* This might seem a straightforward question. If you can restrain yourself from looking ahead or looking at a map, first try guessing the answer using the recommended four-point protocol. Think of all the things that would lead to a low estimate. Realistically, what is the lowest plausible value? Think of all the things that would lead to a high estimate. Realistically, what is the highest plausible value? On balance, what is your best guess? Lastly, how sure are you that the interval you created encloses the truth?

Implicitly, we asked for the shortest distance. If we were to travel west from Los Angeles, circumnavigating the globe, the distance would be about 40,000 kilometres. Beyond this initial *shortest distance* assumption, other uncertainties arise. We might use a map and a ruler to measure the distance. But which map? 'Projecting' the three-dimensional globe that represents the earth onto a two-dimensional piece of paper produces a map. All map projections distort the three-dimensional surface in some fashion. There is no single 'correct' way of doing it. Some maps preserve area, others preserve distances between specified points, and some simply try to make things look about right.

Here are some of the reasonable responses given by individual people:

- *It's [approximately] 400 miles, and it takes about six to eight hours to drive there depending on whether you take breaks.*
- *Six to seven hours by car, depending on traffic and how often you stop.*
- *The trip takes approximately six hours following the speed limit driving straight through … take the I-5 up because it has a faster speed limit (70) than the 99 (55–65).*

Here are some responses returned by various websites:

- *383.8 miles* (by car, MapQuest)
- *5 hours, 34 minutes* (by car, Google Earth)
- *8 hours* (by bus, Greyhound)
- *347.16 miles* (by air, Mapcrow)
- *558.68 kilometres* (by air, Mapcrow)

These answers make it clear that the question was grossly underspecific, ambiguous and context-dependent. We didn't specify if we were asking for the estimate in units of time or distance. We didn't specify which distance units. And we didn't indicate the mode of travel. Seeing the variety of answers helps us to revise the question and remove ambiguities.

We can rephrase the question to ask: what is the shortest distance between Los Angeles and San Francisco, in miles, by road? Now, we have two reasonable answers: '383.8' and 'approximately 400'. The question is still vague, because it allows imprecision and borderline cases.

We can rephrase again. What is the shortest distance between Los Angeles and San Francisco, in miles, by road, to the nearest mile? We finally have what we think is a well-conditioned question. This question may do a little better under the clairvoyance test.

However, despite our efforts, hidden ambiguities and contexts may remain. For example, someone may know a shortcut that requires an off-road vehicle. Certainly, some elements of the question are underspecified. We trust web-based sources to provide a precise answer, but usually the sources don't specify the start and end points of the measurement. They could be general reference points agreed by geographers to represent the centres of the cities, or perhaps from central post office to central post office, or even from one city boundary to the other. Different definitions will give different answers.

Even when asked simple questions, usually we don't see the ambiguities or alternative contexts. Instead, we provide the first thing that occurs to us. This is akin to Daniel Kahneman's idea of thinking fast. We don't think to query the question. Nevertheless, several answers to the question, *how far is it from Los Angeles to San Francisco?* anticipated the ambiguities and provided conditional information. They said it depends on traffic, which route you take, and how often you stop, and then provided an interval or an imprecise answer. These responses are more informative than the precise answers from the web-based applications.

By eliciting intervals in this way, we resolve some linguistic uncertainty and record the expert's lack of knowledge about the quantity. In other circumstances, you may want to have an expert's estimate of the natural variability in a quantity.

The distances between two cities and the number of jellybeans in a jar don't vary much over time, but other important things do. Quantities such as the severity of earthquakes, the amount of rain that will fall next year, the rate of spread of diseases and the price of houses are difficult or impossible to predict exactly, even with relatively complete information, but we may know quite a bit about how variable they are. This information allows us to rule out at least some events as very unlikely, and to consider the expected value of decisions.

Assume for a moment you work in a national park in the United States, say, between Los Angeles and San Francisco, since I've already got you thinking about that part of the world. You're responsible for managing a threatened bird and you need to know how many birds remain. You ask the local bird expert how many there are.

Of course, having read about the methods above, you might ask the expert using the four-point question format. You'll be aware that linguistic uncertainties may arise and craft the question to accommodate as many of these as you can anticipate, and then trial it on colleagues. You put the revised question to the expert who provides you with an interval estimate of the number of birds in your national park at present.

You are also interested in how much the population is likely to vary from year to year, naturally. If the population is relatively stable and you intervene by improving their habitat, you might expect to see an increase in the number of birds. However, if the population fluctuates wildly because of rainfall, fires or the inherent randomness of breeding success you may find it difficult to detect a response, even if the intervention is successful.

This will lead to a different line of questioning. However, the process is essentially the same as the process above. First, identify a clearly defined quantity, such as average annual variability. Define it unambiguously and specify context. Then, put the question to the expert in a structured format. In the case of the bird, you might ask for a statistical representation of variation, such as a standard deviation of population size. But if the expert is not familiar with the concept, you could ask for a related and more intuitive quantity, such as the range of population sizes you would expect to see over (say) ten years.

There are many other approaches to eliciting numbers that make good sense in particular circumstances.[13,14] Many aim to gain enough information to fit a statistical distribution.[15] One of the most common approaches is to ask people to provide '90 per cent credible bounds'. As we have established, this means the person should be 90 per cent sure that the true value lies inside their interval.

For example, economist Sandra Hoffman and her colleagues asked experts to provide 90 per cent credible intervals for their estimates of the risks of food-borne pathogens.[16] The format of the question in their study would take relatively little time to ask, and

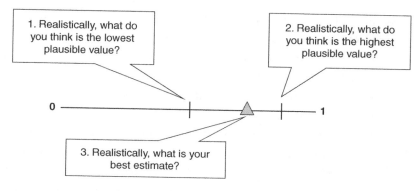

FIGURE 4.3 The three-point format for questions about probabilities.

likely less time to respond to, compared with the four-point format. But the cost of this shorter method is eliciting 90 per cent credible intervals that are too narrow. A four-point procedure probably would have resulted in the experts providing better calibrated intervals, but would take a bit longer.

STRUCTURED QUESTIONS FOR PROBABILITIES

Questions that involve probabilities of events require the expert to form an opinion about the likelihood of an event within a specified time frame or under defined circumstances.

As I mentioned in the last section, my colleagues and I recommend a question format for eliciting probabilities analogous to the four-point format outlined above. The main difference is that it requires only three questions (Figure 4.3). It is not necessary to provide the confidence associated with the interval here (the fourth question) because the quantity is already on a probability scale (0 to 1, or 0 to 100 per cent). The width of the uncertainty interval indicates how sure the expert is in their estimate.

Like the four-point format for quantities, the expert's bounds from the three-point questions do not need to be symmetric around their best guesses. Also, like the four-point format, we ask for the bounds before asking for the best estimate, to get people to think about the extreme values. We preface the first two questions with statements that urge people to think about evidence that points in one direction, and then the other. We ask them to *think about all of the data and reasons why the value may be small. With these in mind, realistically, what do you think is the lowest plausible bound?* We preface the second question with the equivalent conditions.

Questions about probabilities are interesting because they embody uncertainty in the location of the interval and the width of the interval. Consider the question when you throw a coin: *will I throw a head?* It is both a difficult and an easy question. It is difficult in the sense that there's no way to predict the outcome. It is easy in the sense that we're sure that there's no way to predict the outcome and we know the probability of the alternatives almost exactly. Realistically, no amount of additional information will improve our estimate.

Our interval for the answer might be, the chance of throwing a head is [49 per cent, 51 per cent] (meaning the true probability of the event is somewhere between 49 per cent and 51 per cent), to account for the possibility of a slight bias in the coin. We can test our answer by tossing the coin many times, recording the number of heads, and dividing by the number of throws.

Let's try a more challenging example. Imagine you are an intelligence analyst. You want to know, *will the leader of this country resign or otherwise vacate the office of President before 1 April (of some year)?* You consult your country expert. Of course, the expert is unable to give a definitive answer. They say it depends on many political and economic factors. There's no way to be sure. Besides, what do you mean by 'resign' or 'vacate'? What if she's assassinated, dies of a heart attack, or just gets sick? What if she is defeated in an election but retains power by force? What if it's not clear whether she's in power or not? And do you mean the beginning or the end of the day on 1 April?

The original question is overlain by linguistic uncertainty, just as were the questions about quantities in the examples above. You consult other colleagues and revise the question, to clarify meaning and context. You may come up with the following.

For 'yes' to be the outcome, events must not only occur but also be reported by the media prior to the deadline. The leader will be considered President as of this date and time, unless one of the following conditions occurs prior to the deadline:

a) She has died.

b) She vacates or is forcibly removed from the capital/head of government office (or residence) following resignation of office or electoral defeat.

c) She is reported to have vacated the capital in a manner characterised as fleeing the capital, being driven from the capital, or going into exile.

d) She has disappeared from public view, such that it is unclear whether she is alive or whether she is residing within the nation she governs.

e) She is deemed to be in a prolonged or permanent state of mental incapacitation (e.g. coma, vegetative state).

- For condition (a) the question can be closed and resolved immediately.
- For condition (b) the question will be closed when the leader vacates office/power is transferred. Neither tendering of resignation nor electoral defeat is sufficient.
- For conditions (c) through (e), we will observe a three-week waiting period between the condition's occurrence (e.g. date she is reported as going into exile) and the question's resolution. If this or one of the other conditions (c) through (e) still holds at the end of this period, or if other relevant conditions – e.g. condition (a) – are fulfilled prior to the end of the period, the question will be resolved at this time as 'she is no longer in power'.

BBC News or Reuters or Economist Online (<www.bbc.co.uk/ news/> or <www.reuters.com> or <www.economist.com>) will be used for question resolution, or other sources as needed (e.g. CIA World Factbook, Wikipedia), provided those sources do not directly contradict concurrent event reporting from BBC News, Reuters, or Economist Online. If nothing is reported in these sources, then the 'status quo' outcome will be assumed (e.g. the leader has not resigned/vacated office). In cases of substantial controversy or uncertainty, we may refer the question to outside subject-matter experts or may deem the question invalid/void. 'Before' should be interpreted to mean at or prior to the end (23:59:59 ET) of the previous day.[17]

As before, hidden ambiguities may remain. But assuming your expert is happy that the question is sufficiently well defined, you then ask:

- First, consider all the factors that make this event unlikely. Realistically, what do you think is the lowest probability of the event?
- Second, consider all the factors that make this event likely. Realistically, what do you think is the highest probability of the event?
- Finally, on balance, what is your best guess for the likelihood of this event?

Let's say that your expert answers with three numbers: [1, 5, 30]. This says that the expert believes the lower and upper bounds for the probability of the event are 1 per cent and 30 per cent respectively, and their best guess is 5 per cent.

In other words, the expert is saying that he believes it is relatively unlikely that the leader will vacate the office of President by the nominated date. Considering all the evidence supporting the argument that she will leave, the highest probability they can realistically imagine is 30 per cent. If they consider all the evidence against her vacating the office, the lowest probability they can imagine, realistically, is 1 per cent.

In a sense, the best estimate is the expert's judgement of the fundamental uncertainty regarding the event. The bounds represent how sure he is of his estimate of the probability of the event. The interval between the lower and upper bound is the expert's lack of knowledge about the inherent uncertainty.

Importantly, this situation is nothing like tossing a coin, even though we treat it in the same way. There is only one country of interest and it has only one leader. We can't run the experiment many times to validate the answer objectively. Thus, the estimate the expert provides is a credible interval, a subjective belief of the kind we discussed in Chapter 2.

We can make more use of the analogy between long-run frequencies of repeated events and subjective beliefs. When you ask the expert to estimate the probability of an event, you might ask him to interpret this as a bet, although first be sure that the person does not have cultural or religious objections to gambling. If he continues with the task, his subjective probability is reflected in the odds he would accept for a gamble on the outcome of the event; an idea that dates at least to Laplace in the 1800s.[18] The procedure works as follows:

- Give the expert a ticket and say that it is worth a reward (say, $100) if the event, E, occurs.
- Then, offer the expert a reward (in cash, X), payable immediately, for the ticket.
- Begin with a small value for X and increase it slowly until a point is reached at which the person is willing to part with the ticket (this is called the point of indifference). The point of indifference is termed the selling price, X_S.

If the person is rational, $X_S < \$100$. Even if he views the event as certain, $100 now is more valuable than $100 at some time in the future. The person's estimate of the probability of the event is his selling price divided by the reward (in this case, 100).

However, people sometimes exhibit irrational behaviour when confronted by bets, even if they have no ethical objections. A propensity to gamble can cloud judgement, and people are willing to lose money to support what they believe to be true.[19] Statisticians have devised a technique called the reference lottery strategy, which theoretically avoids problems with gambling behaviour.[20] Such tools have been used for applications as diverse as deciding the trajectories of two Mariner spacecraft by NASA.[21]

Interestingly, it turns out that the amount that most people are willing to spend to buy a ticket is less than their belief in the outcome. In contrast, if they already own the ticket and you try to buy it from them, the price at which they would sell it is higher than their buying price, and higher than their belief in the outcome. People tend to value the ticket more highly if it is already in their possession.

We call the interval between the buying and selling prices the expert's region of indifference for the gamble.[22] It is roughly equivalent to the plausible bounds that we elicit with the three-point question format. Statistician Peter Walley calls this interval an 'imprecise probability'.[23]

Intervals have been used for some time to convey uncertainty. For example, in the 1970s, under the guidance of the statistician John Tukey, the Impacts Committee of the US National Academy of Sciences concluded that if the release of chlorofluorocarbons continued at 1977 levels, there was a 50 per cent chance that atmospheric ozone depletion would eventually reach 10–23 per cent. The committee was 'quite confident' (translated as equivalent to 19 chances in 20) that depletion would be in the range 5–28 per cent.[24]

Decision-makers may demand precise estimates, even when no such certainty exists. However, uncertainty has advantages. In negotiations, people can trade expected value for surety, providing a negotiator with an additional dimension in which to seek agreement. Decision-makers can make appropriately risk-averse or risk-seeking decisions. And decision-makers may prefer to know that expert estimates are uncertain. For example, psychologist Nate Dieckmann and his colleagues[25] found, that when evaluating intelligence forecasts, decision-makers tended to give higher levels of credibility to forecasts that reported ranges than to those that provided only point estimates.

USING WORDS FOR PROBABILITIES

I gave an example above in which Sherman Kent noticed that the words used by intelligence agencies to describe probabilities of geopolitical events in the 1960s were interpreted wildly differently, yet everyone assumed everyone else's interpretation was the same as their own. This was a perilous state of affairs, especially when the US Administration of the time was contemplating important decisions such as whether or not to invade Cuba.

Words are used from time to time to represent quantities or probabilities. They provide an order, which is ideal if an order is all that is required. For example, David Vose, an analyst with considerable experience in engineering risk assessments, proposed the following list:[26]

Almost certain
Very likely
Highly likely
Reasonably likely
Fairly likely
Even chance
Fairly unlikely
Reasonably unlikely
Highly unlikely
Very unlikely
Almost impossible

The order in the list reflects relative probability. The expert is asked to choose a phrase that equates best with each event.

Of course, a problem with these lists is that people interpret the words differently, as Sherman Kent discovered. In addition, sometimes the order of the words is not self-evident. It may be difficult to know, for instance, in the absence of the ordered list above, which of the expressions *fairly unlikely* and *reasonably unlikely* denotes a larger probability. I have seen an expert assessment that used the words *scant* and *minor* for the probabilities of a range of events, without defining which word was the higher probability.

In the late 1960s, NASA followed examples set by the US military and adopted 'risk assessment tables' to assist in setting priorities (Table 4.1). The objective was to create assessments that were more reliable than those conducted subjectively and without any guiding principles. Reliability was judged by the repeatability of the results. The 'hazard probability rank' was a verbal description of the relative likelihood of the event. Likelihood categories ranged from frequent or continuous to improbable. Each term was linked to an imprecise

Table 4.1 *Elements of the NASA risk-assessment table*[27]

		Hazard probability rank	
Level/scale	Description	For an individual item	For fleet or inventory
A	Frequent	Likely to occur frequently	Continuously experienced
B	Probable	Will occur several times in the life of an item	Will occur frequently
C	Occasional	Likely to occur at some time in the life of an item	Will occur several times
D	Remote	Unlikely but possible in the life of an item	Unlikely, but can be expected to occur
E	Improbable	So unlikely it can be assumed it may not be experienced	Very unlikely, but possible

quantitative description, so that 'probable' meant 'will occur several times in the fleet or inventory'.

The US intelligence service took this strategy a step further. Sherman Kent pioneered the use of tables that related 'words of estimative probability' to numerical scales (Table 4.2). His idea was to reduce the arbitrary linguistic uncertainty that arises when such words are used in isolation. I provide two examples, one from the US Intelligence Service (Table 4.2) and another concerning climate change risks (Table 4.3).

Words are used differently in the two systems. While we may not agree with the usage (up to 10 per cent probability for something that is 'almost impossible' may seem odd), it is clear what is meant. Linguistic uncertainties may be modelled numerically with a range of approaches.[30] In some circumstances, verbal representations of

Table 4.2 *Kent scale used by the US Defense Intelligence Agency in 1980*[28]

Expression	Synonyms	Rank	Per cent probability
Near certainty	Virtually certain, highly likely	5	91–100
Probable	Likely, chances are good, we believe	4	61–90
Even chance	About even	3	41–60
Improbable	Probably not, unlikely	2	11–40
Near impossibility	Almost impossible, a slight chance, highly doubtful	1	1–10

Table 4.3 *Kent scale recommended by the Intergovernmental Panel on Climate Change (IPCC) to communicate about climate change risks.*[29] *Note that this scale uses overlapping intervals. The IPCC recommends that, when there is sufficient information, it is preferable to specify the full probability distribution or a probability range (e.g. 90–95 per cent) without using the terms in this table*

Expression	Rank	Likelihood (per cent probability)
Virtually certain	7	99–100
Very likely	6	90–100
Likely	5	66–100
About as likely as not	4	33–66
Unlikely	3	0–33
Very unlikely	2	0–10
Exceptionally unlikely	1	0–1

quantities may be more easily understood than numerical values,[31] but in general I recommend that, at the very least, quantitative probability intervals be shown alongside descriptors. Ideally, analysts and experts should reason with numbers, even when data are unavailable and the numbers represent beliefs.

BEYOND QUESTION FORMAT: CONTEXT, INTERACTION AND ANALYSIS

The three- and four-point question formats can be applied face-to-face, by email, using spreadsheets, web-based software or virtually any other means of interaction. In many situations, experts will not be familiar with structured question formats. Some people initially find the process unnecessary or even counterintuitive, in which case they resist participating. It is usually a good idea to go through the details of the elicitation process, answer technical questions, and to run a few trial questions, before embarking on the questions that matter.

The number of questions can restrict the mode of interaction. People become tired after about three hours of direct questioning. It can take an hour simply to reconcile linguistic uncertainty in a single question, before commencing the estimation steps. Face-to-face elicitation is effective if the number of questions is modest, usually no more than about 20 to 30, and the expert is available for the better part of a day.

It may be more effective to distribute questions and give people time to think about answers, gather data, contact professional networks, consider alternative scenarios and make calculations. For example, my colleagues and I emailed a spreadsheet containing as many as 114 questions[32] to ornithologists to assess the conservation status of Australian birds. We used international criteria that include thresholds for population sizes, occupied areas, rates of decline and so forth. The experts spent two weeks thinking about and answering the questions. They found the task challenging but tolerable. It would have been difficult or impossible to collect this much information in a face-to-face meeting.

We may want to gather more information from an expert than a simple interval for a quantity. I described briefly above how you might think about extracting information about the variability of a quantity. If we were interested in even more detailed descriptions of the expert's knowledge, then we would deploy other, more time-consuming and sophisticated techniques.[33]

How hard should the analyst try?

Unfortunately, I should say at the outset that there is no known answer to this important question. The imperatives for finding an answer, any answer, can be powerful or overwhelming. How does the quality of expert information deteriorate as experts tire, and how hard should the analyst try to elicit an estimate once an expert becomes reticent?

If an analyst fails to secure an estimate, then it may be that he or she lacks the necessary skills. But experts sometimes make estimates just to be helpful, to retain the semblance of expert respectability, or because they have been browbeaten into providing an answer. If the analyst tries too hard, the answers may be too unreliable to be useful.

Expert fatigue may corrupt expert knowledge or make it inaccessible. Many concepts are complex. They may involve numerous functions and tens or even hundreds of parameters. There may be several plausible alternative scenarios. Time is limited, the process is demanding, and people tire of estimation.

The balancing act for the person undertaking the elicitation involves keeping the experts within the domain of their knowledge, and putting aside sufficient time to determine where those limits lie – for example, by using test questions (see the next subsection). The region of overconfidence, between the subset of facts experts have learned and the subset they think they know, varies between experts.

Decision analyst Robin Gregory describes[34] his own participation in everything from a two-hour session to reconcile decisions about bus schedules, to elicitations that have taken many weeks, when the context involved multibillion dollar decisions about nuclear power plants. Almost certainly, the effort and time required will depend on decision stakes, the problem's complexity, and differences in the personalities and competencies of the experts involved. In any case, tolerance to inaccuracy will depend on the context. At least part of the answer should lie in the importance of the question.

In general, there is a powerful and unacknowledged tension between the analyst's desire to elicit a value and the expert's reticence to do so. It is easy for the analyst to stray into the expert's region of overconfidence. The only way to be sure you have not overstepped the mark is to validate predictions.

Testing experts and measuring performance

Legal tests to determine the admissibility of expert opinion evidence use a combination of credentials, technical 'knowledge' and reputation,[35] reflecting conventional notions of expertise. The opinions of an expert may be tested by cross-examination, or by the opinions of other experts. Opinions may be 'impeached' by proof that, on a former occasion, an expert expressed a different opinion.

Roger Cooke[36] spent many years evaluating the reliability of engineering estimates. He pioneered the idea of using data to measure expert knowledge objectively. Essentially, he advocated asking experts for facts, a subset of which are known to the facilitator but not to the experts (for instance, facts from recent case studies, experiments, hypothetical scenarios or simulations). He recommended using the results of these tests to evaluate knowledge, weight opinions or exclude some opinions altogether.[37]

The prospect of doing this raises challenging questions. Who sets and administers the tests? Which elements of expertise should the tests examine? Where do the data come from to validate the answers? How does one overcome the reality that experts who are unused to being challenged may be reluctant to be tested? These tools have been deployed and many of these hurdles overcome in applications in law, meteorology and engineering.[38]

Training and feedback

If people are trained, and have the opportunity to learn how to improve their ability to estimate and predict, their performance generally improves.[39,40] The best way to improve judgement performance over time is to develop procedures to involve people routinely in making predictions, and provide them with feedback that compares earlier assessments with outcomes.[41]

Training could involve teaching or refreshing experts on common jargon and theoretical concepts. It may employ case studies, experiments, hypothetical scenarios and simulations to illustrate processes relevant to the questions at hand. It may include numerical and graphical output derived from similar assessments and different ways of representing uncertainty and probabilities.[42]

In some situations, there may be few or no opportunities for feedback. For example, there are few clear parallels for predictions for the social, environmental or health impacts of an emerging technology (e.g. nanotechnology). The success of predictions may not be known for decades.[43] Alternatively, one may develop training and test questions based on hypothetical scenarios and simulations, or generate training materials from data that are otherwise difficult to locate for individual experts (e.g. unpublished results[44]).

While training and feedback generally improve expert performance, bias and overconfidence about facts may persist. Practice and experience alone do not necessarily remove biases. Improvement is usually slow, and a large number of similar assessments are needed to generate substantial improvement. Feedback protocols have been deployed in engineering risk assessments in Europe, but it has taken many years to establish accepted procedures.[45] Even though improvement is not instantaneous, systematic feedback is the most important factor demarcating domains in which expertise develops and improves over time (e.g. chess playing, weather forecasting) and domains in which it does not (e.g. psychotherapy).[46]

CONCEPTUAL MODELS

Models are abstractions. They represent how we think the world works. We build models to answer specific questions and to assist us in making decisions. The type of model we choose – and its complexity – reflects the decision, the available time, and knowledge.

Conceptual models often are useful during expert engagement. Generally, analysts distribute background information prior to eliciting expert estimates. It may include a conceptual model that outlines the scope, context and assumptions of the problem at hand. More commonly, conceptual models are created – or at least, revised – during the elicitation procedure itself, to generate a comprehensive picture of the problem or question.[47] Eliciting conceptual models places special demands on experts because they have to integrate data and ideas about systems, and map processes of cause and effect and their uncertainties.[48]

A diagram is the simplest form of a conceptual model. Figure 4.4 shows the thinking of a hydrogeologist about the source and fate of toxic chemicals on a disused factory site in Italy. The diagram communicates several issues, including importantly the spatial scale of the problem and the level of detail (at least, the detail captured at this stage of problem formulation). It represents conceptual compartments, including factories, tanks, soil layers, groundwater layers, and groundwater movement. Soil composition and discontinuities such as clay caps and the boundary of the permanent aquifer are important in understanding the movement of the two classes of chemicals.

Influence diagrams are useful for developing and exploring ideas because they represent ideas in a flexible form. Shapes (ellipses, rectangles) represent variables, data and parameters. Arrows link the elements, representing ideas about cause and effect among system components. The figure defines processes and pathways by which materials and energy flow through the system.

The example in Figure 4.5 shows that, as land is cleared of vegetation, transpiration rates decline. The water table rises, mobilising salt from the soil profile as it moves. Agriculture can affect river flow rates by modifying direct runoff and by capturing water in dams. Water quality depends largely on agricultural practices and is defined in terms of pesticides and herbicides. Soil condition is a function of farm animal densities and their access to the river.

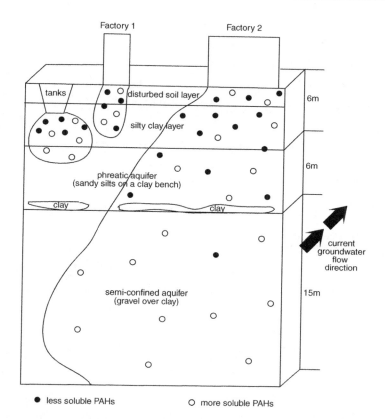

FIGURE 4.4 Conceptual model of the hydrology of a disused industrial site in Italy and the movement of a plume of polycyclic aromatic hydrocarbons (PAHs) from factories into groundwater and to adjacent sites.[49] The model was used to develop ideas for building quantitative models to estimate risks of off-site contamination.
Source: adapted from Carlon et al. (2001).

Often, experts have strong opinions about cause and effect relationships. Their opinions frequently diverge, both among experts and between experts and other stakeholders. We can use alternative conceptual models to show competing ideas about how a system works or how best to manage a situation. Ideally, elicitation processes involve the experts (conventionally defined) *and* stakeholders in developing and revising conceptual models.

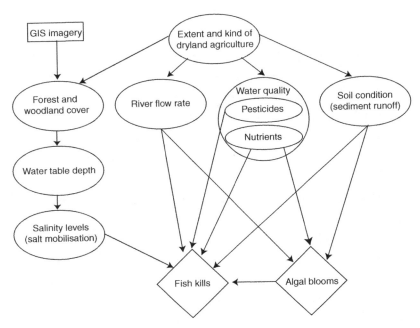

FIGURE 4.5 Influence diagram showing conceptual relationships among system components in a freshwater catchment.[50]

How do you go about sorting through different possible models? One of the main difficulties is the sheer number of alternative ideas. When biologists investigated large numbers of fish dying in the Neuse River Estuary in the US, they found that poisonous algae (called *Pfiesteria*) accompanied the floating fish.[51] People speculated that the poisonous algae killed schools of fish. But there were other possibilities. The dead fish may have been killed by something else, and the algal cells simply prospered in the water conditions created by the dead fish. Lastly, the co-occurrence could have occurred by chance. It is possible, for instance, that the poisonous algae were present elsewhere, or even everywhere, in the estuary. These alternatives are summarised in Figure 4.6.

If we have just two variables, numbers of dead fish and concentrations of poisonous algae, and there are no other factors involved,

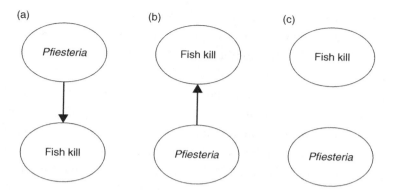

FIGURE 4.6 Alternative fish kill models. Model (a) assumes that blooms of toxic *Pfiesteria* arise of their own accord and then kill fish. Model (b) assumes that dead fish stimulate the formation of toxic *Pfiesteria* from algae that happen to be present at the site.[52] Model (c) assumes that the occurrence of *Pfiesteria* and dead fish are independent.
Source: adapted from Borsuk et al. (2003), and Stow and Borsuk (2003).

then there are four possible relationships between them (including a double-headed arrow, not shown in Figure 4.6). If we have three variables, there are 64 possible relationships. If we have four variables, there are 4,096 possibilities. The number of possible interactions increases very quickly as the number of variables increases.[53]

The search for the right structure is often intuitive. The analyst asks questions about causes, effects and actions that will prevent effects. They search for variables that moderate or enable effects, synergies and interference between variables, and so on. Often, elicitation draws on conceptual models constructed previously. Some differences of opinion about causal relationships may be resolved by theory or data.[54]

Model-based assessments are especially error prone when they require experts to judge outcomes of complex models, when the context is unfamiliar or the quantities involved are very large or very small[55] such as catastrophic failure of a system, extreme weather, coincidences of independent events, and so on. Sometimes, it may be possible to compare the situation with other low-probability events that are better defined. Alternatively, it may be possible to disaggregate the rare event into a sequence of more likely events that are easier to estimate, the combination of which generates the outcome in question.[56,57]

Disaggregation (decomposition) involves reducing a complex and unfamiliar problem to a set of underlying, simpler and more familiar processes,[58] which should, in turn, result in more reliable estimates. Each element in the system should become tangible and easy to envisage.[59] For example, if we look again at the influence diagram in Figure 4.5, we can isolate the link on the right-hand side between soil condition (sediment runoff) and algal blooms. It may look to be a straightforward relationship, but when we ask an expert to quantify it, we may soon realise that it's more complicated than first thought (a common situation in expert elicitation). We could decompose the relationship further by identifying the subprocesses. In this case, it might include turbidity, nutrients and light. Higher sediment runoff increases the concentration of nutrients in the water, which is generally favourable for algal blooms. On the other hand, higher sediment runoff also increases turbidity, which decreases the penetration of light through the water column, creating conditions that are generally *not* favourable for algal blooms. Our submodel captures more of the complexity than was shown in the original link. It is, however, easy to overdo the decomposition and make the problem harder. Complex conceptual maps start to look like bowls of spaghetti. There are many ways to decompose a problem, and analysts should look for one that experts are comfortable with.[60]

Roger Cooke described an experiment from the 1980s in which engineers from ten countries built fault trees for a feedwater system for a nuclear power plant.[61] Each team made an independent estimate of the probability that the system would fail. The experiment was conducted in four stages to examine the influence of different data and different conceptual models on the estimates of failure.

Each team undertook an analysis of the data and independently made point estimates for the failure probability. The teams met and

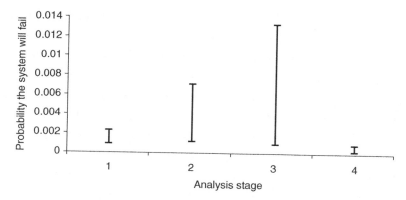

FIGURE 4.7 Range of estimates from ten teams of the probability that a nuclear feedwater system will fail.[62] Stage 1: Qualitative estimation. Stage 2: Estimate based on independent conceptual models and independent data. Stage 3: Common (agreed) model and independent data. Stage 4. Common model and common data.
Source: adapted from Cooke (1991).

discussed their differences. Each group produced a conceptual model (in the form of a fault tree) and made a second estimate. In the third stage they agreed on a model between teams, but used the data they had collected independently to assess the problem. In the final stage, the groups used the same data and the same model. The results are shown in Figure 4.7.

Clearly, different ideas about the logical structure of a problem can contribute to substantially different estimates. Similarly, differences in data collection and interpretation may also influence ideas of cause and effect. The analyst should resolve linguistic differences and other misunderstandings, and then test ideas against data and theory. Remaining differences may be represented in the form of two (or more) diagrams. As in the treatment of expert judgement of facts, it would be a mistake to submerge residual, honest differences of opinion in a consensus or an average model. Residual differences should be reported and their effects on decisions evaluated.

The detail in a conceptual model often depends on the knowledge of the people involved. Engineers assessing the environmental risks of a new port facility will spend a great deal of time breaking down and evaluating the likelihoods of failures in things such as pumps, structures and storage facilities. A hazard such as a spill affecting marine fauna is likely to be treated as a single hazard.

If ecologists join the team, they are likely to lump engineering structures into a few crude baskets. They will, however, be preoccupied by ecological detail. For example, when biologists were asked to assess threats to marine turtles from pollution, nest predation, and fisheries catch, they displayed bias towards creating more detail and weighing more heavily the things they knew most about.[63] The more experience an expert had with a specific hazard, the higher she scored the impact of that hazard, compared to other potential hazards.

People have opinions about the outputs of models, as well as the inputs.[64] It is common to have people revise their estimates of parameters once they have seen the consequences of their beliefs. It is difficult for people to integrate parameters through complex functions intuitively. When this is done explicitly, the results may be viewed as impossible or unlikely, forcing a revision of the parameters or of the functions that link them. While some analysts resist the revision of judgements based on knowledge of the result, it may be an important benefit. Revision embodies learning.

Teams with broad technical expertise are less likely to overlook something that matters.[65] Model uncertainty is difficult to quantify and impossible to eliminate. The only way of determining how appropriate a model is for prediction is to validate it by comparing predictions with outcomes. Treat models as plausible alternatives, and accumulate evidence over time to eliminate unsupported or implausible ideas.[66]

DISCIPLINE IS WORTH THE EFFORT

The above suggestions may seem complicated or time-consuming. After all, you may have relied on experts for years, and have done so just by asking the best person available to you. Or you may be an expert yourself, and be used to dispensing advice regularly. The message is the same. The worst thing you can do, from the perspective of the person seeking advice *or* the person giving it, is to seek or provide unaided subjective estimates about facts or predictions for the outcomes of events from an individual expert.

It may seem laborious and costly to adopt a more structured and comprehensive approach to elicitation, but ultimately, you will waste more time and money without one, unless the answer is self-evident, or the objective is to have an authoritative opinion, and the facts don't actually matter much. This may be a valid social process in some cases, but it's not the point of this book. In circumstances in which facts matter, and insofar as they exist, the prescriptions above will serve to improve the accuracy and calibration of expert judgement, reduce bias and increase reliability.

5   The wisdom of crowds revisited

In the midst of writing this book, a friend from philosophy pointed out that Aristotle argued that the estimates of a large group that includes non-experts should outperform those of an individual expert. Specifically, Aristotle said, '*[i]t may be argued that experts are better judges than the non-expert; but this objection may be met by reference to (a) the combination of qualities in the assembled people (which makes them collectively better judges than the expert), and (b) the fact that in some cases laymen are in as good a position to judge as experts. ... when there are many, each has his share of goodness and practical wisdom; and, when all meet together, the people may thus become something like a single person, who ... may also have many qualities of character and intelligence*'.[1] This view is surprisingly close to the wisdom that emerged from the last 100 years of experiments and observations on group behaviour and expert judgement.

Mathematician Francis Galton opened a can of worms when he wrote a short paper in 1907 entitled *Vox populi*.[2] He described a weight-judging competition held at the West of England Fat Stock and Poultry Exhibition. An unfortunate ox was selected. Competitors bought stamped and numbered cards for 6 pence each, on which they wrote what the ox would weigh once it had been slaughtered and 'dressed'. About 800 cards were sold.

Galton, pre-empting subsequent research into the psychology of motivational biases in expert judgements, noted: '*[t]he judgements were unbiased by passion and uninfluenced by oratory...the six penny fee deterred practical joking and the hope of a prize and the joy of competition prompted each competitor to do his best*'.

Regarding expertise, he observed, '[t]he competitors included butchers and farmers, some of whom were highly expert in judging the weight of cattle; others were probably guided by such information as they might pick up, and by their own fancies. The average competitor was probably as well fitted for making a just estimate of the dressed weight of the ox, as the average voter is of judging the merits of most political issues... '.

It turned out that the median (or middle value) of the 787 valid estimates was 1207 pounds, whereas the correct weight was 1198 pounds, an error of just 0.8 per cent (Figure 5.1). Galton selected the median as the best estimate because of its democratic properties; the majority of people would regard every other estimate to be either too high or too low.

Psychologist Kate Gordon conducted an experiment similar to Galton's in 1924.[3] She asked 200 people to arrange ten objects from lightest to heaviest. She compared the ranks of their individual estimates with the true order, and the average correlation was 0.4. When she averaged the ranks of ten judges chosen at random, the

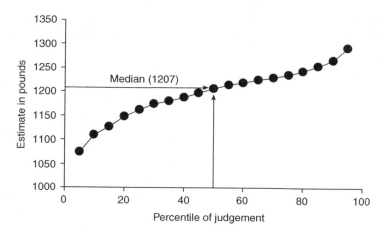

FIGURE 5.1 The distribution of guesses for the weight of a dressed ox published by Francis Galton in 1907.[4] The correct weight was 1198 pounds.

correlation between their ranks and the true order was 0.79. For 50 judges chosen at random, the correlation improved to 0.94.

Galton's and Gordon's prescient experiments precipitated thinking about how groups might perform better than individuals. It might seem counterintuitive that this could be so, but consider Figure 5.2. In this example, even though occasionally an individual judgement is closer to the truth than is the group average, the group averages are consistently reliable. Over many questions, the group average often will outperform the best-regarded person in the group, and the best-performing individual, as it does in this example.

Group estimates of facts are generally more accurate than individual estimates.[5,6] The world's interest in this fascinating topic was stimulated by James Surowiecki's book, *The Wisdom of Crowds*.[7] However, they provide no guarantee of accuracy. For instance, Facebook's Twitter crowd, which included venture capitalists and industry insiders, predicted that the first-day closing price of its shares

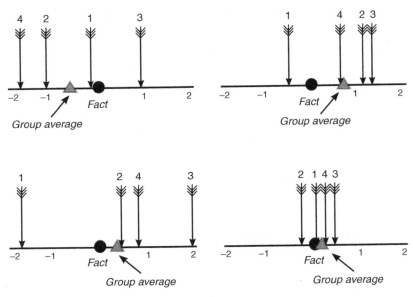

FIGURE 5.2 Hypothetical example of four experts each making estimates of four facts. This figure looks like one in Chapter 2, but here I have added each group's average.

on the stock market would be $54. The crowd's prediction was nearly $16 above the closing price of $38.60.[8] While this group estimate was inaccurate, it was still an improvement over most lone voices.

If groups are generally better than individuals at estimating quantities, might they be better than individuals at more complex tasks? Scientists at Microsoft Research[9] explored different mechanisms for encouraging people to solve IQ-style questions in groups of different sizes. Groups of more than two generate important improvements in problem-solving ability, although the marginal gain began to decline beyond a group size of about five. Groups composed of ten average people (with IQs of 100) performed at a level equivalent to someone with an IQ of 126. There was additional gain for every person added (Figure 5.3).

Can groups handle even greater complexity? The answer is, yes. In mathematics, the Fields Medal is equivalent to winning a Nobel Prize. Recent Fields Medallists Terry Tao and Timothy Gowers

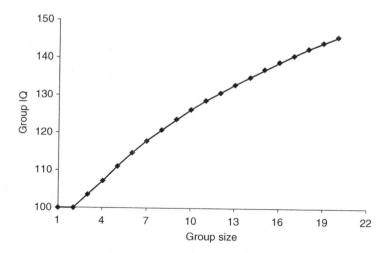

FIGURE 5.3 Microsoft researchers[10] explored the potential of groups to solve mentally challenging IQ tasks, and recorded the marginal increase in in-group IQ with each additional worker. Performance improved with every person added, although maximum gain per person was around four or five people. Pairs of people did not improve performance over individuals because one answer was selected at random when the results disagreed. Source: adapted from Kosinski et al. (2012).

developed a web-based system that allows anyone to contribute solutions to problems too hard for Fields Medallists to solve in isolation.
They called it the PolyMath project.[11]

They began by trying to find a solution to a problem called
the Hales–Jewett theorem. There was a proof but it was difficult to
follow and they wanted to find a simpler one. Imagine that you are
colouring the squares in a grid. What percentage of the squares can
you colour before you are forced to make a straight line of colours
along a row, column or diagonal? The Hales–Jewett theorem provides
an answer. Finding a new solution took just six weeks, lightning fast
in mathematical time.

Two computer scientists analysed the contributions to the new
solution.[12] Amateurs, some of whom had never published a scientific
paper, contributed many critical steps (Figure 5.4).

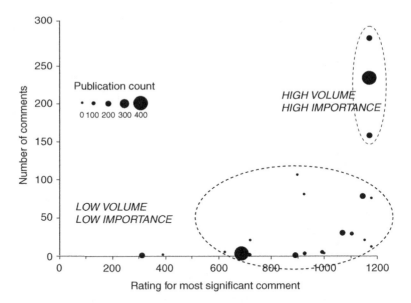

FIGURE 5.4 Contributions to the solution of the first PolyMath project.
Scores for the number of comments and the importance of contributions
towards the solution of the Hales–Jewett theorem. Several critical
contributions came from people with few publications (<100), who
ranked low on professional seniority and who made just a few comments.
Source: adapted from Jacob (2011).[13]

Researchers in chemistry tried a similar strategy, putting a long-standing problem on the web. The crystal structure of a protein (M-PMV retroviral protease) had withstood many attempts to resolve. They turned the challenge into a game called 'Foldit' and encouraged consortia of players to try to solve their problem.[14] At least two groups of players were successful. The refined structure was published in 2011 and it provides new insights for the design of drugs.

There seems to be no end to the creative and practical advantages of using groups to make estimates and solve problems. So when do groups go awry? We saw in earlier chapters that sometimes all experts in a group are systematically biased in a particular direction. Framing, anchoring, availability bias, motivational bias and other psychological and contextual factors may also affect groups, as they do individuals.

Yet, the things that make groups smart are not the same as the things that make individuals smart. The ability of groups to work effectively and solve problems is associated with qualities such as social and cultural diversity, the social sensitivity of group members, the equality of group discussions, and larger proportions of females.[15] It is not determined by qualities such as average individual IQ or the maximum IQ of any member of the group.

Ideally, expert groups should be as diverse as possible, and systems for engagement should encourage people to listen and integrate information and reasoning from as many sources as possible, and to explore competing explanations.[16] The basic idea is that groups made up of individuals with diverse experiences, backgrounds and contexts will draw on different sources of information, form independent initial estimates and avoid shared professional myopia. They will not anchor on common points nor be motivated by common personal goals.

DEALING WITH GROUPS OF EXPERTS

Strong personalities in groups influence outcomes. People defer to others they believe have greater authority or who appear confident, even when asked to make an independent estimate. Participants advocate positions, views are anchored and change is resisted. People hold covert opinions, and there is pressure to conform. Some analysts do not acknowledge these problems and continue as if group estimation is largely detached from subjective influences – even for circumstances as value-laden, uncertain and politically charged as assessing radioactive waste risks.[17]

The traditional way of dealing with a group of experts is to herd the group into a room and ask, *what do you think?* The group mulls over the question in an unstructured way and forms a consensus. I term this 'naïve group judgement'.

This approach is perhaps the worst possible technique.[18] It exposes participants to the countervailing pressures listed above. It leads to groupthink, a process in which arbitrary starting positions and the hidden agendas or prejudices of a few lead a group to a position that does not reflect the individual participants' private opinions.[19]

Groupthink can be very difficult to avoid, even in institutions devoted to estimation and prediction. The US Senate investigated the assessments that led to the US invasion of Iraq in 2003.[20] One of the most strident beliefs among the intelligence community before the invasion was that Iraq harboured weapons of mass destruction (WMD). We now believe that their assessments were wrong.

The Senate Committee Report noted that the intelligence community suffered from a collective presumption that Iraq had an active and growing WMD program. The Committee concluded that this 'groupthink' dynamic led intelligence community analysts to interpret ambiguous evidence to indicate the presence of a WMD program and to ignore or minimise contrary evidence. The Senate report went on to say that intelligence managers '*did not encourage analysts to challenge their assumptions, fully consider alternative arguments, accurately characterize the intelligence reporting, or counsel analysts who lost their objectivity*'.[21]

Richards Heuer, an intelligence analyst in the CIA and the US Department of Defence for more than 50 years, commented on the Senate Committee report.[22] He argued that occasional surprises are inevitable and cognitive limitations are inescapable. His view was that the conclusions of the Committee were a case of hindsight bias. Analysts start with assumptions – often about foreign capabilities and intent – that have been developed through education, training and experience. These assumptions inevitably form a mindset that influences what information the analyst sees and what information is judged reliable and relevant.

Think about what the analysts knew:

- Saddam Hussein had mounted unprovoked attacks against Iran and Kuwait.
- He had been defeated and humiliated by the United States and its allies.
- He claimed to be a missile threat to Israel.
- There was no credible evidence that Saddam's hostile intentions had changed.
- Israel blocked Iraq's clandestine program to build a nuclear weapon by bombing its Osirak nuclear facility in 1981.
- Later in the 1980s, Iraq used chemical weapons against Iran and against its own people.
- After the 1991 Iraq war, analysts discovered that they had underestimated Iraq's inventory of WMD. They did not want to make the same mistake again.
- After 1991, weapons inspectors found and destroyed significant stockpiles of WMD, including 40,000 chemical munitions, 500,000 litres of chemical weapons and 1.8 million litres of precursor chemicals.
- Inspectors did not believe that they had found all the stockpiles.

As a consequence, analysts had a strong and seemingly well-justified mindset that Saddam had WMDs and would eventually use them.[23] The predisposition was not overridden by subsequent information that ran counter to it.

Establishing the reliability of clandestine information is excep-tionally difficult. Heuer documented a case by a colleague who researched 68 cases of surprise and deception in military operations between 1914 and 1968. He found ten cases in which clandestine sources gave detailed military plans to an enemy prior to an intended military attack.

In half of these cases, the plans were carefully fabricated decep-tions, while the other half were genuine breaches of security. The fabricated plans were accepted as genuine in all five cases, while the genuine plans were rejected as fabrications in four of the five instances – an overall failure rate of 90 per cent.

To counter the inevitable blame game that follows intelligence 'failures' – even in circumstances in which we know outcomes are inherently unpredictable – and to counter the many psychological and contextual biases to which we may be susceptible, we need struc-tured processes to deal with experts, together with dispassionate and repeatable measures of their successes and failures.[24] In Chapter 4, I described structured elicitation procedures to anticipate and miti-gate some of the most important and pervasive psychological and motivational biases in individuals. Additional procedures, tailored to a group context, can help us to get the most out of groups.

Some of the earliest, and still among the most useful, of these tools are the Delphi and related techniques.[25] They were developed by the RAND Corporation in a joint US Air Force/Douglas Aircraft initiative in 1948[26] to overcome groupthink and the influences of dominant individuals.[27]

In these approaches, all participants make an initial estimate of a fact. In the standard Delphi technique, the collective estimates and associated reasons behind each are anonymously shown to all experts, who then make a second, private estimate of the fact. The process can be repeated if desired. The technique is defined by ano-nymity, iteration, controlled feedback and statistical aggregation of results.[28] Figure 5.5 summarises the operations for estimating simple quantities.

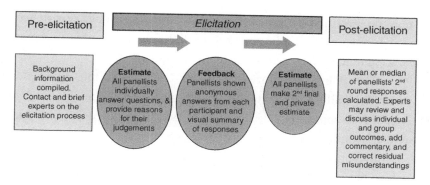

FIGURE 5.5 Summary of the Delphi group estimation process.[29] During the feedback period, we diverge from standard Delphi procedures by encouraging individuals to discuss estimates and consider alternative explanations. Tetlock, Mellers and colleagues have used similar approaches very successfully.

We call our adaptation of the Delphi method the IDEA protocol (for Investigate, Discuss, Estimate, Aggregate). In it, experts are given the opportunity to discuss differences of opinion following their first estimates,[30] allowing people to reconcile the meanings of words and context, thereby removing arbitrary language-based disagreements.[31] Throughout the process, they weigh the opinions of others, integrate new information, improve understanding of the question, and evaluate the context and motivations of other participants, before arriving at their final estimate.

Vigorous peer review and debate, including cross-examination of competing claims, assists decision-makers to synthesise evidence and improve estimates.[32,33] However, discussion may lead people to declare their identity to others, exposing them to dominant opinions and the pressure to conform. This possibility can be managed by a skilled facilitator, and is at least partially mitigated by the fact that the second estimate is strictly anonymous.

This process works best when, as noted above, people from a variety of social contexts and 'positions' in a debate are involved, providing a measure of protection against motivational bias. Experts may be stratified by geography, technical background, experience, affiliations or other relevant criteria. Individual contributions may be weighted by their performance on test questions.

The IDEA procedures described here are simple to implement. Typically, participants respond positively to being involved in Delphi-like approaches.[34,35] Figure 5.6 shows the outcomes of group deliberations on two geopolitical questions.

In some circumstances, analysts use Delphi techniques to reduce between-expert variation iteratively so that they can arrive

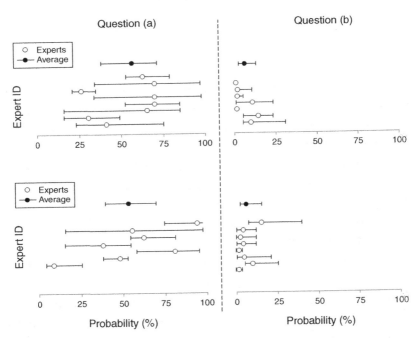

FIGURE 5.6 Two groups estimated the probability of the outcomes of two geopolitical questions. The correct answer for question (a) was 'yes' (100 per cent), and for question (b) was 'no' (0 per cent). The group average estimates for the probabilities of these events were reasonably similar between groups, despite substantial disagreement within groups. Source: adapted from Wintle et al. (2012).[36]

at a 'consensus' position.[37] In other applications, and in the modified IDEA approach that we recommend, analysts retain differences of opinion.[38]

IDEA groups may be run in a very wide range of operating modes, from face-to-face interactions[39] to a process run by a facilitator who moves between experts who never see one another, or even know who else is involved. Other alternatives include phone- or web-based interactions, or deliberations based around facilitated email communications.[40] These modes accommodate different locations of experts, forms of communication and time frames. The general approach is inexpensive and requires little in the form of technical overheads or support. IDEA groups are best for acquiring instantaneous estimates, rather than continuous assessments. It can be difficult to maintain a small group's enthusiasm for a single question over prolonged periods.

Delphi methods are also easy to apply poorly, if the basic prescriptions for iteration of estimation and anonymity erode. When poorly applied, they have been criticised for limiting interactions between experts, dealing inadequately with uncertainty, encouraging uniformity and discouraging dissent. They are not ideal for examining complex systems because participants may not have the opportunity to discuss important interactions and the joint probabilities of coincident events. Discussion aimed at resolving differences may fuel expert overconfidence.[41]

There are many variations on the basic theme of estimate–feedback–estimate that underpins our IDEA protocol. As noted above, the critical features are diverse group composition, the initial private estimates, active consideration of alternative data and ideas,[42] and the anonymity of final estimates.

There are also other, effective models for eliciting group estimates that diverge from this general approach. One can simply poll a large number of people (say, on the internet), eliminate clearly irresponsible or extraneous answers, and find the average of the remaining estimates. This was essentially Francis Galton's approach to estimating the weight of a dressed ox. Other approaches such as the 'Nominal Group Technique' use a combination of group inter-action (usually, discussion) and voting.[43]

In the 1980s, political scientists and economists began to experi-ment with market-based approaches for obtaining collective answers to questions. The basic idea is that a person seeking an answer sets up a market and encourages people to trade shares that represent their predictions. In theory, the share prices reflect the collection of all the public and private information possessed by all the traders about future events.[44] People who correctly predict the value of the quantity or the outcome of the event are rewarded. Those who are wrong are penalised.

Consider creating a market for a political event. We specify a binary event, such as *'Will a Scottish referendum make Scotland independent of the United Kingdom before January 1, 2015?'* and create a contract for the event 'yes'. After the outcome was observed, the contract would have paid $1 (in this example) if Scotland had voted to become independent. It paid $0 (Figure 5.7).

If you look at the IPredict market for this question on January 24, 2014, the value of a $1 contract for the affirmative position was about $0.11. That is, the market had reached a consensus that the chance of the event was 11 per cent. If you believed that the prob-ability of the event was higher than that, you should have bought a contract because you would expect to make money. Conversely, if you believed the chance was less than 11 per cent, you should have wanted to sell any shares you had.

People can buy and sell such contracts. Several companies have set up markets for many such questions. This intriguing innovation is based on the premise that, with appropriate rewards and a system for making trades, markets will integrate public and private information efficiently. The University of Iowa created one of the first prediction markets, for a US election in the 1980s. Prediction markets experi-enced a setback in the early 1990s. Economist Robin Hanson set up a

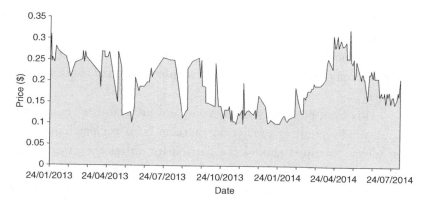

FIGURE 5.7 IPredict market for the question, '*Will a Scottish referendum make Scotland independent of the United Kingdom before January 1, 2015*'. The Price axis is the market value of one share, and a contract is $1 per share. The site indicated '*This contract will close at $1 if a Scottish referendum held to make Scotland Independent of the United Kingdom passes before 1 January 2015. Otherwise the contract closes at $0*'. Thus, the price is equivalent to the market's belief (the probability) that Scotland will vote for independence.[45] The figure shows the daily opening price. Source: www.ipredict.co.nz; accessed: 6 August, 2014.

market to predict sociopolitical events, funded by the Department of Defense. US Senators criticised the initiative, claiming that it would encourage people to try to make money from assassinations and terrorist attacks.[46] There are now several policy analysis markets that offer futures on such events.

Information markets are still relatively new, and there are several unanswered questions about their use:[47] how is the performance of the system related to the psychology and decision biases of individuals? Individuals might have large incentives to conceal or misrepresent what they know. If markets are thin (the number of participants few), how will the performance of the system be affected? How can we find the people with the relevant information and have them participate?

All expert groups occasionally get things wrong. If participants are misinformed about a topic and share information, then the process may reinforce biased estimates. Occasionally, methods are applied poorly, and groups become susceptible to many of the same factors that compromise naïve group interactions. Markets may respond slowly to new information if there are few traders.

However, prediction markets are not just 'crowds', comments Hanson. The point of prediction markets is to get participants to self-select. Investors should not participate unless they think they know more than other participants, and those who actually do know things will make money, forcing less knowledgeable investors out of the market.[48]

Several experiments have compared the accuracy of quantitative estimation tasks of prediction markets and Delphi techniques to other approaches, including traditional meetings and the Nominal Group Technique. While some studies find only small differences between different structured methods, in general, structured techniques such as Delphi groups and prediction markets provide answers that are more accurate than do unstructured meetings.[49] Prediction markets may be particularly effective at tracking group opinion about processes or events over time. Figure 5.8 shows the results of estimates for the outcomes of geopolitical events for the period 2012–2013. The unweighted linear opinion pool (a crowd opinion) was least accurate (higher Brier scores are worse). The IDEA groups and the prediction market substantially outperformed the simpler, crowd-sourced estimates.

AGGREGATING OPINIONS

The easiest way to avoid conflicting opinions is to ask just one person. Larger sets of experts mean greater possibility for divergence. Stratifying the sample of experts to include a range of demographic and social attributes will further increase the chances of disagreement. I take the view that such disagreements – if they are not based on arbitrary linguistic differences – are an essential element of good

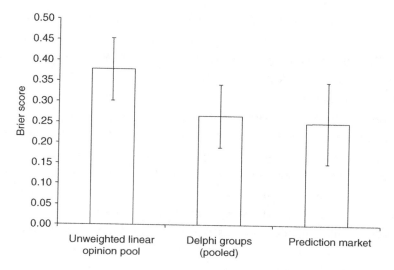

FIGURE 5.8 Average accuracy of several IDEA expert groups and a prediction market for geopolitical questions that resolved between September 2012 and March 2013, compared to a crowd-sourced, unweighted pool of expert predictions.[50] The y-axis is a measure of the accuracy of these methods (the average Brier scores). Smaller Brier scores are more accurate. Error bars are 95 per cent confidence intervals. Source: adapted from Wintle et al. (2012).

group judgements. Group diversity generates relatively accurate and well-calibrated answers.[51,52]

If we acknowledge that expert judgements typically are better than non-expert ones, and that the notion of expertise should be broadened to include people who do not fit the conventional mould but who may have valuable knowledge and experience, then perspectives from a broad cross-section of people with relevant exposure to the problems may provide a relatively reliable estimate or prediction. This, in turn, suggests that it may be important to further stratify the experts by their interest in the outcome.

Stratification of the pool of experts is a critical step in the selection process. As noted above, some dimensions include social context, motivation (personal or professional interest in the outcomes), technical background, gender and culture.[53]

For example, an international group was formed by the World Health Organization to examine the potential for microbiological pathogens to contaminate food.[54] The opportunity to participate was advertised. Selection criteria included technical expertise, professional recognition (panels, editorial boards, conferences), publications, the ability to participate in group discussions and ability to draft clear reports. Experts were selected from the set of candidates to ensure representation from organisations, geographic regions, genders and levels of economic development.

It is rarely possible to arrive at complete agreement between experts, even given extensive discussion and reassessment. However, combining disparate opinions raises several difficulties, principally because there is no single, 'right' way of combining multiple expert opinions.[55] There are, however, some wrong ways to do it.

For example, the United States Nuclear Regulatory Commission asked 12 experts to estimate the average frequency with which pipes of a particular kind might rupture. Their estimates ranged from 5×10^{-6} to 1×10^{-10} (Figure 5.9).

The government report concluded that the failure rate was 1×10^{-10}, which is equal to the lowest value estimated by any of the experts.[56] That is, the government interpretation was the same as the most extreme (lowest), single-expert estimate. Eight of the 12 experts provided estimates of failure rates higher than the upper 95th quantile of the government summary. These results suggest that in-house government experts interpreted the experts' estimates post hoc. There was no indication that the in-house estimates were based on better data.

The final recommendation had much narrower uncertainty bounds than the spectrum of expert advice (see Figure 5.9), especially considering the log scale of the failure rates, and the fact that experts were not asked for bounds. The final aggregated answer of all the experts' opinions indicated that pipe failure would be more frequent than was outlined in the final recommendation. A sceptical mind may ask whether the cost of more robust pipes required as a result of

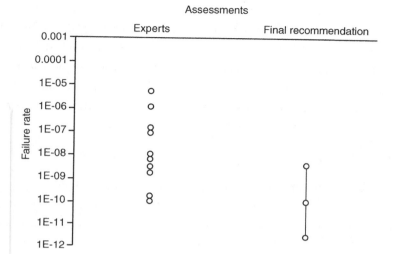

FIGURE 5.9 Comparison of expert estimates and final recommendations for pipe-failure rates in a nuclear facility. The lines joining points under the final recommendation link the 5th and 95th quantiles. Source: adapted from US Nuclear Regulatory Commission, 1975, in Stewart and Melchers (1997, p. 87).[57]

more frequent ruptures weighed on the minds of those making the final assessment. It may be that the final recommendation was supported by independent, empirical data, but even with the best intentions, decision-makers, like experts, are susceptible to motivational biases – such as being swayed by project costs. Subjective aggregation is generally not defensible. However, there's no way to know, yet, who was right and who was wrong in these assessments.

In many situations, the average or median of a group of expert estimates will provide a reliable summary (sufficiently accurate, unbiased and well calibrated).[58] One should be careful, however, not to lose sight of differences of opinion. The extreme values may be the ones that get things right. Rather than throw them away, they should be integrated into discussion – to at least determine whether someone has good reason for providing an extreme value. Perhaps they know something that other people don't.

Consistency of opinions among experts may be interpreted as a measure of reliability. Alternatively, differences may reflect honest, valid differences of opinion. The way in which the analyst handles differences should reflect a coherent philosophy about the nature of the uncertainties and the ways in which they affect decisions. There are two basic forms of aggregation: numerical and behavioural aggregation. The following sections outline their forms and uses.

Behavioural aggregation

Consensus among experts arises in several ways. As noted above, unstructured deliberations are susceptible to groupthink. An alternative is to use structured group meetings to find a consensus estimate. Most structured behavioural approaches involve experts first expressing and presenting their views to others. Facilitators then assist experts to discuss their positions, and to revise their assessments as linguistic hurdles are overcome and information is shared.[59]

A range of approaches from philosophy[60] recommend that facilitators deconstruct the logic of arguments and describe clearly the evidentiary support for opposing viewpoints (using conceptual models; see Chapter 4). These tools are better suited to debates about complex issues than for the estimation of narrowly defined facts, although group consensus has been used to estimate facts in a few instances. For example, the International Whaling Commission used group consensus to develop estimates of important variables for the recovery of Bowhead whales.[61]

Initially, experts advance a series of claims. They are subject to rebuttal by other experts. Disagreements are about facts, theories or principles (different scientific traditions or differences of a metaphysical or ethical nature). Disagreements about data are the easiest to resolve, whereas disagreements about scientific theories or ethics are the most difficult. Facilitators identify and treat sources of disagreement[62] by resolving logic, identifying data, examining the extent of support for alternative explanations and so on. The logic of discussion can be displayed on argument maps.[63]

Finally, facilitators seek 'closure' or 'resolution'. Closure may be achieved through:[64]

- Sound argument: a 'correct' position is identified and opposing views are seen to be incorrect.
- Consensus: the experts agree that a particular position is 'best'.
- Negotiation: an arranged resolution is reached that is acceptable to the participating experts and that is 'fair' rather than correct.
- Natural death: the conflict declines gradually and is resolved by ignoring it, usually because it turns out to be unimportant.
- Procedure: formal rules end sustained argument.
- Resolution: including eliminating, mitigating or accepting differences of expert opinion.

Closure assumes that expert estimates provide a rational interpretation of evidence and that 'political' influences can be divorced from the scientific process. Of course, experts are not completely rational. In general, closure is not guaranteed and it is not always sensible to seek it. Disagreement may reflect important, legitimate differences of opinion. Group consensus may lead to overconfidence and polarisation of opinions in which groups adopt a position that is more extreme than that of any individual member.[65] Agreement does not always reflect shared knowledge, but may instead reflect deference to a scientific consensus that is not justified by data.[66]

It is always useful to eliminate arbitrary elements of disagreement (such as ambiguity and underspecificity). Remaining differences of opinion about scientific detail and ethical issues can be recorded and communicated, without compromising the ability of a group to reach a decision.

Numerical aggregation

Numerical aggregation uses quantitative strategies, rather than behavioural ones, to arrive at a combined estimate. If the information is probabilistic, then the tools of formal statistics are appropriate.[67] In particular, Bayesian analysis can combine knowledge from subjective sources with current information to produce a revised estimate.[68]

Estimates of quantities or probabilities associated with belief may be combined as weighted linear combinations of opinions.[69] Simple averages of individual estimates seem to perform well compared to unstructured, consensus-based estimates when the focus is on unambiguous, value-free and sharply defined parameter estimates.[70]

For example, 15 experts were asked to estimate the total size of the koala population in the state of Queensland, Australia (Figure 5.10) using the IDEA protocol. Their individual estimates were obtained using the four-point elicitation method. Their opinions about their best guess and bounds were rescaled to be consistent 90 per cent intervals. Then the mean and median of their best guesses and upper and lower bounds were used to represent the group's estimate.

Health scientist Rachel Peachy and her colleagues[71] used a similar approach to estimate the effects of plain packaging of tobacco products on smoking in adults and children. They interviewed health professionals in three countries and asked them to predict the decline in the number of smokers two years after the introduction of plain packaging. They averaged the experts' estimates, resulting in an expected 1 per cent decline in smoking among adults and 3 per cent decline among children.

More complicated formulae involve, for example, weighting the estimates differently following discussion among experts or the acquisition of new data,[72] or based on the performance of an expert against a set of known values.[73] Typically, these approaches incorporate an expert's accuracy and confidence. Experts who are routinely closer to the truth and who are relatively confident are weighted most heavily.

Roger Cooke[74] developed a protocol for elicitation in risk assessment called the 'Procedures guide'.[75] It is intended for 'practical scientific and engineering contexts'. Expert judgement is, for him, another form of scientific data. He assumes that some unique, real value exists but that we are uncertain what the value is, so

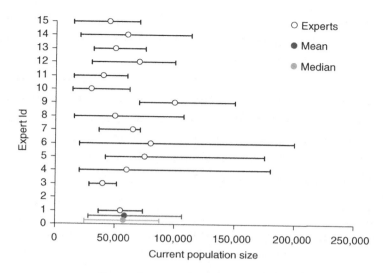

FIGURE 5.10 Best estimates and 90 per cent credible intervals for the size of the koala population in the state of Queensland, Australia, in 2012.

uncertainty may be described by a subjective probability distribution with values in a continuous range.

The method includes the essential elements of the IDEA process described above, and allows question formats such as the three- and four-point formats that I recommend in this book. It includes performance measures that are made known to experts. The goal is to combine expert estimates into a numerical consensus that is transparent, fair, neutral and subject to empirical quality control.

More generally, Cooke[76] recommended that expert judgements should be subject to quality control, usually by validating a proportion of estimates with data. The methods for measuring accuracy, bias, calibration and reliability should encourage experts to state their true beliefs. Lastly, and importantly, weights should be based on performance and not on status or experience.

Most expert groups include habitually overconfident people, those whose spread of estimates is small but accuracy is low compared to other experts. Typically, performance-based weights generate more accurate estimates. The best expert is only rarely better than the performance-weighted group.

There are other ways of attacking the problem of aggregation.[77,78] Many new methods are being developed that straddle the divide between mathematics and psychology, some of which provide objective means for weighting expert estimates against data.[79] In general, they aim to improve the quality of expert judgement and to combine it with data in consistent ways.[80]

WHEN ARE GROUP JUDGEMENTS NOT WORTH HAVING?

Even if, in general, properly managed groups outperform individuals, are there circumstances in which group judgements are poor? And at what point should they be disregarded?

We saw above that Facebook's Twitter crowd overestimated its closing first-day share price. The prediction market InTrade predicted that it was 75 per cent certain that a Supreme Court decision in the US would go one way, and a day later it went the other. People can be quick to call attention to the fallibility of markets. So why bother? As Robin Hanson pointed out, 75 per cent certain means that we fully expect that it will go against the majority position 25 per cent of the time. Getting things wrong in an individual instance does not mean that the approach is not useful.

For really difficult problems, groups won't necessarily provide all the answers. Take, for instance, the following example. Unexploded bombs are a serious problem worldwide. Public health scientist Jacqueline MacDonald asked explosives experts to imagine a scenario in which two children find a mortar bomb and toss it around like a football, dropping it on a hard surface occasionally.[81] She asked them to estimate the probability of an explosion. The scenario is relevant because 1,976 sites in the US are contaminated by unexploded bombs. No amount of clean-up effort can guarantee 100 per cent removal.

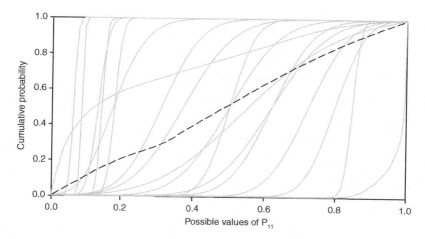

FIGURE 5.11 Experts' fitted cumulative density functions for the chance that a mortar will detonate if handled by children.[82] The solid curves are the estimates of the individual experts, and the dashed curve represents the aggregated mean explosion probabilities estimated by the experts. The horizontal axis indicates the probability of explosion. The vertical axis represents the cumulative probability that the chance of explosion is less than or equal to the corresponding horizontal axis value. Source: MacDonald, Small and Norgan (2008).

The experts had an average of 24 years' experience each in handling explosives. Many were involved in current operations. All but one had military experience and most knew at least one person who had been killed or injured while clearing unexploded devices. MacDonald fitted a statistical distribution to their answers. Their best guesses ranged from close to zero to close to 100 per cent, and the average of their estimates and uncertainties resulted in an almost uniform distribution between zero and 100 per cent, indicating that any answer was roughly equally likely (Figure 5.11). Their group judgement was uninformative.

Just as importantly, if a decision-maker had consulted just one expert, many of them would have given estimates with very narrow bounds, indicating false certainty. That is, they would have been quite sure of their estimates, even though the estimates varied dramatically between experts.

The explosives experts didn't disagree about everything. For example, most of the experts believed that it was virtually impossible for one of the evaluated items to explode under the handling scenario described.

Thus, some questions are hard, even for groups. It is very difficult to know, ahead of time, which questions will make a group stumble. However, all other things being equal, groups outperform individuals consistently and by a considerable margin.

6 Tips to get the best out of experts

Policy-makers are concerned with ensemble judgements. They are obliged to consider all potential sources of uncertainty, including those not examined formally by experts. Some aspects of a decision may be concrete, but almost always, other aspects will be political or intangible. Some may affect policy-makers personally. Decision-makers may be more interested in robust strategies that avoid the worst outcomes, than in trying to maximise expected benefits.[1]

In this book, I treat only the relatively simple problems of how to ask experts about well-defined, unique facts (numbers, quantities, rates, outcomes of events). The facts may exist in the present or they may be realised in the future. Even in these relatively simple circumstances, we need to combat the pervasive weaknesses and unacknowledged myopia that is deeply buried in expert judgement.[2] There are tractable ways to achieve this.

ADVICE FOR DECISION-MAKERS

To improve the judgements we elicit from experts, I recommend that decision-makers and analysts adopt the following rules:[3]

1. Be clear about what you want from experts: estimates of simple facts, predictions of the outcomes of events, or advice on a best course of action.
2. Be clear about the domains of expertise that will help, and choose people whose skills, training or verified experience (where it exists) are squarely in those domains. This may include people who, on paper, don't fit the typical 'expert' mould. Where the opportunity exists, offer appropriate training.
3. Choose as many experts as possible; don't be concerned about their age, number of publications, peer status, technical qualifications or apparent impartiality.

4. If the matter at hand is politically sensitive or socially or emotionally charged, ensure that the experts have diverse relevant opinions or positions. Work to diversify the culture, gender, context and perspectives of the participants. Try to include people who are less self-assured and assertive, and who integrate information from diverse sources.

5. Compose questions to avoid arbitrary linguistic misunderstandings and psychological trip wires such as framing, anchoring, availability bias and so on.

6. Use structured question formats to counter tendencies towards overconfidence, and oblige participants to consider counter-factuals and alternative theories.

7. Use structured, facilitated group interactions to counter dominance effects, anchoring and other factors that lead to groupthink.

8. Provide opportunities for participants to see the opinions of other participants – only after they have made an initial, private estimate. Give the group the opportunity to reconcile misunderstandings and to introduce new information. Ensure that the experts actively seek and consider evidence and arguments that disagree with their position. Then, ask for a second, private opinion from each participant.

9. Weight opinions equally, unless you have proven, documented, unambiguous measures of performance on similar questions, in which case, weight by performance history. Remember that traditional metrics of expertise – age, rank, experience – do not generally reflect expert performance.

10. If the opinions more or less coincide, use the average of the group. If opinions diverge substantially, consider ways of combining or summarising their estimates that retain the breadth of opinions. In both cases, retain and consider the ranges of opinions and uncertainties. Give the experts feedback on their estimates and any weights you applied.

In public policy institutions and businesses, it may be necessary to set up an independent unit to oversee the application of these principles, because most experts will not be led quietly to this context. The pull of status and public expectation are strong, the incentives for overconfidence are pervasive, and most people are unaware of their personal stakes and psychological frailties.

The sentencing to jail of seven scientists for manslaughter in connection with the earthquake that killed 309 people in the town of

FIGURE 6.1 Some of the unanticipated devastation at L'Aquila.
Source: European Photopress Agency.

L'Aquila in Italy in 2009 underlines the importance of ensuring that experts leave uncertainty in plain view, and that their judgements are kept separate from policy decisions (Figure 6.1).[4] In the case, the court ruled that the experts had given '*inaccurate, incomplete and contradictory*' advice about earthquake risk. The experts included six geophysicists and one government official (a hydraulic engineer). All were members of Italy's National Commission for the Forecast and Prevention of Major Risks.[5]

Scientists and the media jumped to the scientists' defence. *The Age* in Australia, and the *Guardian* in the UK, likened the case to the 1633 trial of Galileo, who was coerced by the Vatican to retract his theory that the earth revolved around the sun. The American Academy for the Advancement of Science wrote an open letter to the Italian President, signed by 5,000 scientists, arguing that '*years of research, much of it conducted by distinguished seismologists in your own country, have demonstrated that there is no accepted scientific method for earthquake prediction that can be reliably used to warn citizens of an impending disaster*'.

From the beginning, however, the prosecution had built the case around miscommunication rather than prediction. In a news feature in the journal *Nature*[6] the public prosecutor for the case, Fabio Picuti, was quoted as saying *'I'm not crazy... I know they can't predict earthquakes. The basis of the charges is not that they didn't predict the earthquake.'* Similarly, the journal *Scientific American*[7] cited Dr Vincenzo Vittorini, who lost his wife and daughter, as saying *'All we wanted was clearer information on risks in order to make our choices.'* The point was that the experts made pronouncements that determined behaviours, rather than just describing what they knew. The message communicated by the government official was that there was *'no danger'*, and that he had been assured by the scientific community that *'it's a favourable situation because of the continuous discharge of energy'*.

ADVICE FOR EXPERTS

Many scientists aspire to have their work affect public policy. I believe that substantial social benefits may arise from considering relevant facts and uncertainty, and reasoning carefully around them. Often, however, this perspective is perceived by policy-makers to be academic, unrealistic, issue-driven or just too difficult to understand. To improve the accessibility of ideas and the relevance and credibility of technical inputs, I recommend the following simple rules.

1. *Understand the limits of your expertise.* Most definitions of expertise include skills, training, experience and professional recognition. However, qualifications, experience and confidence are not related to performance on questions of estimation and prediction. Try to compensate the tendency to become overconfident by actively seeking differences of opinion, counter-arguments and challenges from as diverse a group of others as possible. Test your knowledge and seek systematic, critical feedback about your performance. In short, temper judgements with a degree of humility.
2. *Be the right expert.* The fact that you are asked for an opinion does not mean you are the person best placed to provide it.

Decision-makers may not understand fully the problem or the expertise available to them. Decision-makers probably will be optimistic about your knowledge and ability to provide definitive answers. Clarify the expert selection process, express any concerns you might have about your inclusion, and work with the analyst and other experts to identify and fill any obvious deficiencies in skills and expertise.

3. *Join a group.* Judgements based on inputs from multiple experts consistently outperform judgements from a single 'best' expert. Ensure that your group is diverse. Listen and consider seriously the opinions of other experts, including those less well-qualified and less experienced than yourself.

4. *Disclose motivational biases.* Some motivational bias in judgements is unavoidable. If the issue at hand is sharply polarised, declare your position. Recommend that additional experts with competing positions be included.

5. *Resolve linguistic uncertainty.* Look for critical terms and concepts that are underspecified, ambiguous, vague or context-dependent and resolve them by specifying thresholds, defining meaning, providing additional information and describing context. Framing the problem and getting agreement on precise definitions needs to come early in the process, well before any efforts to elicit numbers.

6. *State your knowledge and reasoning.* Outline the reasoning and the evidence that supports your estimate of a fact or quantity, even if you are not asked to do so. Outline alternative hypotheses of cause and effect. Use explicit models, mathematics and data where appropriate.

7. *Don't trust your gut.* Distrust rapid, intuitive judgements. Intuitions should be trusted only when they have been acquired on the basis of appropriate experience conditioned by repetitive, personal feedback. For most settings, where the task requires extrapolating to new tasks or scenarios, you have a greater chance of being correct by working through the problem carefully and documenting your reasoning.

8. *Quantify uncertainty.* Expert estimates often understate uncertainty (overconfidence, excessive precision), provide inadequate or jargon-laden descriptions of uncertainty, or fail to include any uncertainty statement at all. Provide an upper and lower bound around estimates for quantities and likelihoods, even when the analyst doesn't ask for them. These

uncertainties should be retained in the decision-making process, and be presented to the decision-maker along with final and/or aggregated estimates.

9. *Train and practise.* Engage in training, by making and documenting judgements. Practise dealing with a variety of question formats, frames and expert domains, answer test questions and explore the bases for estimation errors.

10. *Solicit feedback.* In the majority of disciplines, experts are not provided with adequate feedback on their performance as part of the task environment. Seek feedback on the actual outcomes of estimates and predictions, whenever the opportunity arises.

Note that these steps address only some of the multitude of issues that may influence judgements in risk-assessment settings. The context of an assessment will influence the extent to which this advice may be deployed. An expert should be mindful of the issues raised above, but limitations will depend on time, budget, political pressures, the mode of interaction (email, workshop, questionnaire response, video conference), and the mode of communication of the advice (informal, verbal advice, an informal report, or a formal, publicly available document). The principles might be applicable in all cases, but the emphasis and the implementation will be quite different.

Expert knowledge remains a valuable resource provided that it is elicited carefully, and with an awareness of potential pitfalls. In the lists above, I have emphasised the importance of scrutiny, actively seeking counter-arguments and data to validate judgements, and looking for opportunities for feedback.

It is the responsibility of the expert to communicate what they don't know. For estimates of facts and the probabilities of outcomes, these uncertainties are captured in the intervals arising from the three-point and four-point question formats described above. More complex and detailed elicitation techniques may result in fully described statistical distributions. Many numerical and visual tools are available for communicating in ways that suit particular audiences.[8]

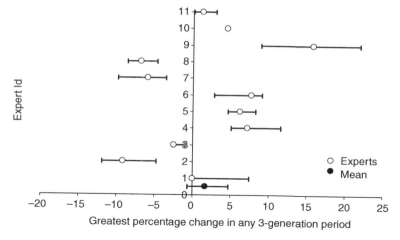

FIGURE 6.2 Group estimates of the rate of change in a koala population over three generations.

Estimates that appear wildly uncertain can still lead to robust decisions. So, as an expert, don't fear that expressing your genuine uncertainty will result in an uninformative or useless judgement. Consider again the example I provided in Chapter 5, where estimates were elicited from a group about koala populations in Queensland, Australia (Figure 6.2). The same group also estimated the rate of change of a koala population. Estimates over three koala generations ranged from declines of as much as 10 per cent to increases of more than 20 per cent. Confronted by such disagreement, especially when the 90 per cent credible intervals don't even overlap, a decision-maker may be inclined to say, we need more data. Scientists, being scientists, would agree.

However, the decision in this situation was whether or not to classify the populations as 'threatened', on the basis of their rates of decline. Figure 6.3 shows three decision thresholds. If the rate of decline is greater than 30 per cent, in three generations, they may be listed as vulnerable. If the rate exceeds 50 per cent they may be listed as endangered. If the rate exceeds 70 per cent they may be listed as critically endangered. Despite their fundamental disagreement about

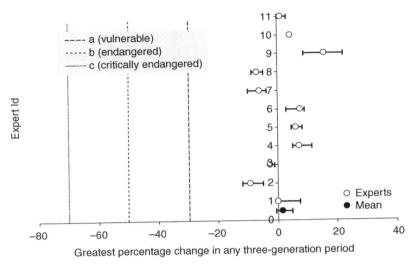

FIGURE 6.3 Group estimates of the rate of change in a koala population over three generations, together with the decision thresholds for the population's conservation status (dashed lines, from left to right, represent critically endangered, endangered and vulnerable).

increases and decreases, all the experts agree that the population is not threatened, at least based on the rate of decline of the population over the last three generations.

THE MYTH OF EXPERTISE

The myth of expertise is that, following appropriate formal training, experts slowly accumulate knowledge over long periods through experience, and that this leads to a gradual improvement in their ability to estimate facts and make predictions.

In fact, some experts acquire skills in a narrow domain, which they can be expected to use reliably. Other experts acquire some understanding of the models, concepts, jargon and data in a slightly wider domain. They may be relied on to make accurate and well-calibrated estimates and predictions in that domain, only if they have practised making such judgements repeatedly, and have received immediate, personal feedback. If experts cannot substantiate claims of expertise by training, experience and a record of clearly defined, unambiguous, accurate prediction, then they should not be uncritically trusted to reliably estimate facts or predict outcomes.

The prescriptions in the lists above borrow from the collective advice of several people whose work I describe in this book: Daniel Kahneman, Amos Tversky, Paul Slovic and their many colleagues advise us to take great care to deal with psychological cues and context. Grainger Morgan laid the foundations for ways in which we might engage with experts to elicit their knowledge. Scott Armstrong describes an entire architecture for forecasting and many sensible guidelines. Philip Tetlock has shown us that, in the absence of direct feedback, experts can be highly credible and yet uninformative. Roger Cooke reminds us that prediction and estimation are empirical matters and that we should test and validate with data to discriminate poor judges from good ones. The lists above reflect my attempt to distil these ideas into an accessible form for the subset of questions that involve simple, well-defined facts.

Policy-makers are faced with more difficult problems, to decide among options or courses of action. Decisions involve matters of fact, as well as matters of value and preference. Most policy decisions do not attempt solely to maximise objective measures of net benefits, although decisions should not conflict unjustifiably with satisfactory or optimal expectations, where the data exist to estimate them. Ralph Keeney, Robin Gregory and their colleagues provide the analytical tools for grappling with these more difficult problems.[9]

In real decisions, costs and benefits are highly uncertain. Often, communication is vague and ambiguous. Misunderstanding and miscommunication of uncertainty can have substantial policy implications. Most people are aware that special-interest groups use experts selectively to find solutions that are best for their interests, often in adversarial circumstances. Stakeholders attempt to manipulate opinion by pandering to psychological biases to channel sentiment and public perception. Framing, visibility, the potential for outrage, the availability of examples, the appearance of control and technical novelty all provide opportunities for people to advance private interests. Political viability of decisions may be bought at the price of scientific rigour, leading to less efficient management of areas such as public health.[10] Once the motivation for stakeholder engagement is defined, the challenge is to develop a mode of involvement without compromising whatever independent evidence may be relevant to making a decision.[11]

The trouble is that many experts are no better at making decisions than are interest groups pushing a self-interested barrow. Both scientists and sociologists have criticised experts involved in policy[12] because it makes the exercise of power by scientists and vested interests acceptable, but may be no more than a collection of selective assumptions, data and assertions – around which the status of the experts creates an aura of unassailable authority.[13]

The alternative is for businesses and government decision-makers to explore options publicly, in understandable language.[14] It is beyond the capabilities of technical experts to anticipate the full range of legitimate points of view, or the full set of ideas about cause and effect. We need partnerships between stakeholders and experts[15] in which the position of the expert is subordinate to the stakeholder. In this context, experts may assist people to critically examine their thinking and to understand the ideas and values of those with whom they disagree. The role of experts, then, is to cross-examine ideas, to collect and present data and to test models relevant to public policy issues, to ensure internal consistency, to eliminate linguistic uncertainty and other sources of arbitrary disagreement, and to clarify the implications of assumptions. Finally, their job is to leave uncertainty and honest disagreements in plain view.

Our reliance on experts fixes our attention on the knowable, leading to over-dependence on fact-finding. Even when scientists recognise the limits of their knowledge, the policy world often asks for more research. Philosopher of science Sheila Jasanoff put it succinctly: '*For most complex problems, ... uncertainty, ignorance and indeterminacy are always present. We need disciplined methods to accommodate the partiality of scientific knowledge ... Humility instructs us to think harder about how to reframe problems so that their ethical dimensions are brought to light, which new facts to seek and when to resist asking science for clarification'.*[16]

Experts suffer from the same human frailties as anyone else. Most aspire to be respected, valued members of society. They too can be self-promoting, greedy, self-deluded or just plain mad. But they may hide behind the mantle of scientific authority and be difficult to question. Some scientific experts believe that they are smarter than (almost) everyone around them, creating an aura of arrogant self-confidence that is difficult to challenge. We cannot expect such people to realise these misdemeanours, especially when, in many circumstances, we encourage this behaviour.

Until we treat expert judgement with the same seriousness as we do data, then the foibles, errors and misconceptions will persist. We should afford to expert opinion the same level of reverence and scepticism that we afford to data, trying just as hard to avoid bias, manipulation and arbitrary, avoidable subjectivity. We should validate judgements where we can, and invest in improved methods for acquiring them.

Endnotes

I WHAT'S WRONG WITH CONSULTING EXPERTS?

1 Welke et al., 2009.

2 See, for example, the European Food Safety Authority, 2011.

3 Meyer and Booker, 1990. Experts are a source for rules and standards (Peel, 2005), they estimate facts, and they contribute to decisions to undertake activities (Gullet, 2000).

4 Spruijt et al., 2014.

5 French, 2012.

6 Solomon et al., 2007. See also Green and Armstrong, 2007.

7 Lawson, 1900, pp. 1–2.

8 US Rules of Evidence 702 (1992; see Imwinkelried, 1993).

9 Imwinkelried, 1993.

10 Kirsch, 1995; Haack, 2001.

11 Lawson, 1900, p. 236. In Australian Federal courts, opinion evidence is admissible if it assists '...*the trier of fact in understanding the testimony, or determining a fact in issue*' (ALRC, 1985, pp. 739–740). Scientific validity is established through falsifiability, peer review, acknowledged error rates, general acceptance of ideas and valid methods (Preston, 2003; Fisk, 1998, p. 3).

12 Stern and Fineberg, 1996.

13 Gustafson et al., 2013.

14 Krinitzsky, 1993; see also Fischhoff et al., 1982.

15 Fischhoff et al., 1982; Speirs-Bridge et al., 2010.

16 *Exonerated by DNA: Massachusetts wrongful convictions overturned*, S. Cowans, November 2011, The Schuster Institute of Investigative Journalism, accessed March 4, 2013, www.brandeis.edu/investigate/innocence-project/Stephan-Cowans.html.

17 *U.S. Will Pay $2 Million to Lawyer Wrongly Jailed*, E. Lichtblau, *New York Times*, accessed March 4, 2013, www.nytimes.com/2006/11/30/us/30settle.html?_r=0.

18 *Exonerated by DNA: Massachusetts wrongful convictions overturned,* S. Cowans, November 2011, Schuster Institute of Investigative Journalism, accessed March 4, 2013, www.brandeis.edu/investigate/ innocence-project/Stephan-Cowans.html. *How far should fingerprints be trusted?,* A. Coghlan and J. Randerson, September 2005, *New Scientist,* accessed January 27, 2007, www.newscientist.com/article/ dn8011-how-far-should-fingerprints-be-trusted.html#.UgMWOBajIbU.

19 Ulery, Hicklin, Buscaglia and Roberts, 2011.

20 Dror, Peron, Hind and Charlton, 2005.

21 Dror and Rosenthal, 2008.

22 *Ibid.*

23 International Monetary Fund, 2006, Chapter 1, p. 1.

24 *Risk Mismanagement,* Joe Nocera, January 2009, *New York Times,* accessed January 6, 2009, www.nytimes.com/2009/01/04/ magazine/04risk-t.html?pagewanted=all.

25 *Ibid.*

26 *The causes and current state of the financial crisis.* Written Testimony of Mark Zandi, Chief Economist and Cofounder, Moody's Economy. com, before the Financial Crisis Inquiry Commission, January 2010, accessed March 10, 2013, www.economy.com/mark-zandi/documents/ FCIC-Zandi-011310.pdf. A collateralised debt obligation is an investment security backed by a set of bonds, loans and other assets.

27 Campbell, 2002.

28 Kunda, 1990; Spetzler and Staelvonholstein, 1975.

29 Benson and Nichols, 1982.

30 For example, Crawford-Brown (1999) defined five categories of scientific evidence for risk assessments:

   1. Direct empirical evidence: direct experimental observation of cause and effect, probability or frequency;
   2. Extrapolation: observations outside the range at hand;
   3. Correlation: statistical associations between measures;
   4. Theory-based inference: relationships and causal mechanisms inferred from understanding of physical or ecological principles;
   5. Expert judgement.

31 Gregory et al., 2012, pp. 26–27.

32 *Ibid.*

33 Krinitzsky, 1993; Shrader-Frechette, 1996b; O'Brien, 2000.

34 French, 2011.

35 Slovic, 1999; see also Johansson, 2002.

36 *Fatal occupational injuries by worker characteristics and event or exposure, All United States, 2008,* Census of Fatal Occupational Injuries (CFOI) – Current and Revised Data, US Bureau of Labor Statistics, accessed March 4, 2013, www.bls.gov/iif/oshwc/cfoi/cftb0238.pdf.

37 Feynman,1986.

38 *Early Space Shuttle Flights Risker than Estimated.* 2011 NASA risk review;www.npr.org/2011/03/04/134265291/early-space-shuttle-flights-riskier-than-estimated; Hamlin, T., Kahn, J., Thigpen, E., Zhu, T. & Lo, Y. (2011) *Shuttle Risk Progression by Flight.* NASA Space Shuttle Safety and Mission Assurance Office, Johnson Space Center, Houston, Texas; http://ntrs.nasa.gov/archive/nasa/casi.ntrs.nasa.gov/20110008208_2011007983.pdf.

39 Source: www.defense imagery.mil/.

40 Feynman, 1986.

41 *Ibid.*

42 Meehl, 1954.

43 Elstein, 1995, pp. 49–59; Berner and Graber, 2008.

44 Meehl, 1954.

45 In another example, expert cardiologists generally do worse than the predictive equations recommended by the American College of Cardiology (Lipinski et al., 2002).

46 Cocozza and Steadman, 1978.

47 Meehl, 1986.

48 Grove and Meehl, 1996; Grove et al., 2000.

49 Statistical methods were defined very broadly to include multiple regression, discriminant analysis, unit-weighted sums of predictors and other mechanical schemes that yield precisely reproducible but not necessarily optimal predictions.

50 For example, Pons et al., 1999.

51 Dawes, 1979.

52 Berner and Graber, 2008.

53 Martin, Quinn, Ruger and Kim, 2004; Ruger, Kim, Martin and Quinn, 2004.

54 Ruger, Kim, Martin and Quinn, 2004, p. 1180.

55 *QuesTec*, Wikipedia, accessed August 8, 2013, http://en.wikipedia.org/wiki/QuesTec

56 Kahneman, 2011; Gilovich, Griffin and Kahneman, 2002.

57 *How to Dispel Your Illusions*, F. Dyson, December 2011, *The New York Review of Books*, accessed August 8, 2013, www.nybooks.com/articles/archives/2011/dec/22/how-dispel-your-illusions/?pagination=false.

58 Grove and Meehl, 1996; Grove et al., 2000.

59 Kahneman, 2011; Gilovich, Griffin and Kahneman, 2002; Engelmann, Capra, Noussair and Berns, 2009.

60 Armstrong, 1980.

61 Graham and Hammit, 1996.

62 Evatts, Mieg and Felt, 2006.

63 Walton, 1997.

64 Gans and Palmer, 2004, p. 244. See also Johnson and Blair, 1983; Walton, 1997.

65 Ezrahi, 1990.

66 Walton, 1997.

67 Walton, 1997.

68 O'Brien, 2000.

69 Evans, 2008; Carr, 2004.

70 Failing, Gregory and Harstone, 2007.

71 Ruckelshaus, Levin, Johnson and Kareiva, 2002, p. 691.

72 Kahan, 2015; see also Kahan, 2013.

73 By Kerr, 1996; also see Kammen and Hassenzahl, 1999.

74 Kerr, 1996, p. 913.

75 See Shrader-Frechette, 1996a, b; O'Brien, 2000.

76 Ball, Maggs and Barrett, 2009.

77 Shuman et al., 1993 in Freckelton, 1995; ALRC, 2000.

78 Wolfgang, 2002.

79 See, for example, Inayatullah, 2008; Armstrong, 2001; Lawrence, Goodwin, O'Connor and Onkal, 2006.

2 KINDS OF UNCERTAINTY

1 Regan et al., 2002.

2 Good, 1959.

3 Lawson, 1900, p. 236.

4 Stephens et al., 1993, p. 272.

5 Kaplan and Garrick, 1981, p. 17.

6 Hacking, 1975, p. 143.

7 Hacking, 1975; Chatterjee, 2003.

8 Hacking, 1975; Colyvan, 2001.

9 *Words of Estimative Probability*, S. Kent and the Board of National Estimates, 1964, Central Intelligence Agency Publication, accessed March 9, 2013, www.cia.gov/library/center-for-the-study-of-intelligence/csi-publications/books-and-monographs/sherman-kent-and-the-board-of-national-estimates-collected-essays/6words.html.

10 See Regan et al. (2002) for more details, and see Anderson (1998), Carpenter et al. (1999) and Wade (2000) for application of Bayesian methods to environmental problems.

11 Hacking, 1975.

12 Hacking, 1975.

13 *Ibid.*

14 Modified from Henrion and Fischhoff (1986) in Morgan and Henrion (1990).

15 Kaiser, 2002.

16 Redrawn from Kaiser, 2002.

17 Vanackere, 1999; Regan et al., 2002.

18 See references in Regan et al. (2002). There are other, better ways to deal with vagueness than attempting to eliminate it, including fuzzy sets which use degrees of membership to deal with borderline cases (see Walley and DeCooman, 2001; Regan et al., 2002a). Regan et al. (2000) suggested their use in classifying conservation status. For instance, a species that has declined by 70 per cent may have partial membership (say 0.25 on a scale of 0 to 1) in the set of threatened species. Species with higher rates of decline should have a higher degree of membership.

19 *Earthquake Facts and Statistics*, Earthquake Hazards Program, USGS, 2013, accessed March 9, 2013, http://earthquake.usgs.gov/earthquakes/eqarchives/year/eqstats.php.

20 *Oil tanker spill statistics*, International Tanker Owners Pollution Federation Limited 2012, 2013, accessed March 9, 2013, www.itopf.co.uk/information-services/data-and-statistics/statistics/documents/StatsPack_001.pdf.

21 *Ibid.*

22 Gigerenzer et al., 2005.

23 Gigerenzer et al., 2005.

24 This definition is limited to calibration of intervals. It ignores calibration for categorical questions and quantitative questions when responses are point estimates, rather than intervals.

25 See Ashton (2000) for more nuanced interpretations.

26 There are several ways to rescale estimates so that they can be compared among questions and among experts. See Cooke (1991); Burgman et al. (2011a).

27 Cooke, 1991; Brier, 1950.

28 French, 2011; French, 2012.

29 For instance, Morgan and Henrion (1990) noted linguistic uncertainty but did not distinguish between its different forms. Klir and Harmanec (1997) nominated vagueness and underspecificity (defined as above) and added conflict uncertainty to their taxonomy. Ben-Haim (2006) used a slightly different interpretation of linguistic and epistemic uncertainty. Some taxonomies confuse epistemic and linguistic uncertainty. Others introduce redundant categories. Many in environmental science treat only epistemic uncertainty (e.g. Chesson, 1978; Shaffer, 1987; Hilborn, 1987; Burgman et al., 1993; Shrader-Frechette, 1996a). Interval probabilities can be assigned to represent an expert's degree of belief where lower and upper bounds encompass the range of beliefs (Walley, 1991). Treatments of subjective uncertainty may use interval arithmetic, imprecise probabilities, Dempster–Shafer belief functions and related tools (see Regan et al., 2002), some of which are outlined in the chapters that follow. In some cases, consideration of even a subset of the full spectrum of uncertainty has been considered to be debilitating. Beissinger and Westphal (1998) argued that there are insufficient data to parameterise models dealing with epistemic uncertainty for all but a handful of species. But there has been no comprehensive evaluation of the importance of the full spectrum of uncertainties for decision-making. Although linguistic uncertainty is common, it is often ignored and only epistemic uncertainty is considered. Clear understanding of the nature of uncertainty will assist analysts to use appropriate methods.

30 Dieckmann, Mauro and Slovic, 2010.

3 WHAT LEADS EXPERTS ASTRAY?

1 The person or team in setting the context of a problem *'defines a set of issues and selects a set of respondents who are experts on the issues'* (Cooke, 1991).

2 Hart, 1986.

3 Hart, 1986; Gullet, 2000; Collins and Evans 2007; Barley and Kunda, 2006.

4 Bernard 1988; Meyer and Booker, 1990.

5 Forrester, 2005.

6 Tetlock, 2005.

7 Burgman et al., 2011b.

8 *Ibid.*

9 Aspinall, 2010.

10 Potchen, 2006.

11 Burgman et al., 2011b.

12 Grove and Meehl, 1996.

13 See also Davis et al., 2006.

14 Cooke, El Saadany and Xinzheng Huang, 2008.

15 Denning, Johnson, Ehrlinger and Kruger, 2003.

16 Kruger and Dunning, 2009.

17 Wintle (2013) found that narrow intervals correlated with accuracy but confidence did not. So, the more indirect measure of confidence (interval width) was a better predictor of accuracy than the direct measure (stated confidence in the expert's answer).

18 Koriat, 2012; Hertwig, 2012.

19 Denning, Johnson, Ehrlinger and Kruger, 2003.

20 Capen, 1976.

21 Morgan and Henrion, 1990.

22 After Mosleh, 1987, in Cooke, 1991.

23 After Christensen-Szalanski and Bushyhead, 1981.

24 After Murphy and Winkler, 1977, 1984, in Plous, 1993.

25 *Risk Mismanagement*, Joe Nocera, January 2009, *New York Times*, accessed January 6, 2009, www.nytimes.com/2009/01/04/magazine/04risk-t.html?pagewanted=all.

26 Figlewski, 1979; Morgan and Henrion, 1990; Plous, 1993.

27 Stern and Fineberg, 1996; Walton, 1997.

28 Johnson and Bruce, 2001.

29 Fischhoff, Slovic and Lichtenstein, 1982.

30 Wright, Bolger and Rowe, 2002.

31 Grigg, 1958; Armstrong, 1980.

32 Luft, 1950.

33 Wise, 1976; Armstrong, 1980.

34 Tetlock, 2006.

35 *Ibid.*

36 Lipinski et al., 2002.

37 Reischman, 2002.

38 Önkal, Yates, Simga-Mugan and Oztin, 2003.

39 See Shanteau (1992b); Slovic (1999); Burgman (2005); Garthwaite et al. (2005); Chi (2006) and Evans (2008) for reviews.

40 Hilgartner, 1990.

41 Sternberg et al., 1993; Wynne, 1996; Beck, 1992; Yearley, 2000; Irwin, 2001; Gregory and Miller, 1998; Leadbeater, 2003.

42 Kahneman and Tversky, 1979; see also Fischhoff et al., 1982; Tversky and Kahneman 1982a; Slovic, 1999.

43 Bernstein, 1996, p. 263.

44 Thaler, 1991.

45 Gregory, Lichtenstein and MacGregor, 1993.

46 Bernstein, 1996.

47 Drawn from Tversky and Kahneman, 1974, 1982a, b; Kahneman and Tversky, 1979, 1984; Fischhoff et al., 1982; Slovic et al., 1984; Plous, 1993; Morgan, 1993; Adams, 1995; Fischhoff, 1995; Morgan et al., 1996; Freudenburg, 1996; Freudenburg et al., 1996.

48 Kahneman and Tversky, 1979, 1984.

49 Tversky and Kahneman, 1985.

50 Tversky and Kahneman, 1971.

51 Englich and Soder, 2009.

52 Slovic et al., 2000.

53 After Slovic et al., 2000.

54 After Slovic et al., 2000 and Gigerenzer, 2002.

55 See Meyer and Booker (1990); Vose (1996) for discussion.

56 *Shark attack statistics.* http://oceana.org/en/our-work/protect-marine-wildlife/sharks/learn-act/shark-attack-statistics. Accessed October 25, 2013.

57 Lamb, B., Baughman, C., Keynes, S., Moylan, S. and Tomlinson, D. 2005. *Shark attacks: myths versus reality*. Flinders University, South Australia. [online] http://furcs.flinders.edu.au/education/med_stud/y2/posters/2005%20HMF%20sharks.pdf. Accessed March 13, 2013.

58 Neff and Hueter, 2013.

59 *The cost of a false-negative decision about an emergency call*, D. Goodsir and L. Kennedy, June 7, 2001, *The Age*, Melbourne.

60 French, 2011.

61 Bier, 2004.

62 Gigerenzer, 2002.

63 *Ibid.*

64 After Gigerenzer, 2002, p. 125.

65 Gigerenzer, 2002, p. 14.

66 In addition, known background frequencies of an event are sometimes ignored in favour of new information. It was base-rate neglect and was first demonstrated in the famous 'cab-problem': (Bar-Hillel, 1980).

67 See Goldring, 2003.

68 Plous, 1993.

69 See Tufte (1997) for a discussion of the way evidence was used in the decision to launch the Challenger.

70 Deffenbacher, 1980; Fulero, 2009; Perfect, 2004.

71 Cooke, 1991.

72 Van der Heijden, 1996; Cooke, 1991.

73 Fischhoff, Slovic and Lichtenstein, 1982; Moore and Healy, 2008; Speirs-Bridge et al., 2010.

74 Modified from Ayyub (2001) and Burgman (2005).

75 Freudenburg, 1999, p. 108.

76 Freudenburg, 1999; Ayyab, 2001.

77 *Ibid.*

78 Bier, 2004.

79 Wagenaar and Keren, 1986.

80 Berner and Graber, 2008.

81 Vose, 1996.

82 Krinitzsky, 1993.

83 Kruger and Dunning, 2009.

84 Taylor and Brown, 1988.

85 Johnson and Fowler, 2011.

86 Nordhaus, 1994, in Kammen and Hassenzahl, 1999.

87 After Nordhaus, 1994, in Kammen and Hassenzahl, 1999, Fig. 4.3.

88 Moore et al., 2010.

89 Mullainathan, Noth and Schoar, 2012. We need to be especially wary when experts' motivational biases run contrary to our own. Economist Sendil Mullainathan and his colleagues arranged for auditors to meet with expert financial advisers and present different types of portfolios. Some of the portfolios were in line with the financial interests of the advisers (e.g. returns-chasing portfolios) and others ran counter to their interests (e.g. portfolios with company stock or very low-fee index funds). Advisers often gave advice contrary to the interests of their clients, encouraging returns-chasing behaviour and actively managed funds that had higher fees, even if the client started with a well-diversified, low-fee portfolio.

90 Dommelen, 1999; Munnichs, 2004.

91 Gigerenzer, 2002.

92 *Ibid.*, pp. 20–21.

93 Slovic, 1999; see also Rohrmann, 1994, 1998; Weber et al., 2002; Kalof et al., 2002.

94 Slovic, 1999; see also Rohrmann, 1994, 1998; Weber et al., 2002; Kalof et al., 2002.

95 Slovic, 1999.

96 Soll and Klayman, 2004.

97 Barber and Odean, 2001.

98 Fischhoff, 1994; Slovic, 1999.

99 Bian and Keller, 1999a, b.

100 Hayakawa et al., 2000. Most Japanese believed they were worse than average drivers and needed collision insurance, even though there is no law requiring it. In contrast, most American drivers believed they were better than average drivers. In America, drivers are required by law to have collision insurance.

101 Kahneman, 2011; Gilovich, Griffin, and Kahneman, 2002; Gigerenzer et al., 1999.

102 Evans, 2008; Glimcher and Rustichini, 2004.

103 Armstrong, 2006; Hogarth, 2005.

104 Kahneman, 2011; Gilovich, Griffin and Kahneman, 2002.

105 Kruger and Dunning, 2009.

106 e.g. Goldberg, 1965; Athanasopoulos and Hyndman, 2011; Jamtvedt et al., 2006.

107 Brooks, 2007.

108 Winkler and Poses, 1993; Hogarth, 2001; Chi, 2006.

109 Laughlin and Ellis, 1986.

110 Todd and Gigerenzer, 2007; Gigerenzer, 2007.

111 Berlin, I. (1953) *The Hedgehog and the Fox*. Weidenfeld & Nicolson, London.

112 Lewandowsky and Kirsner, 2000.

113 *Ibid.*

114 Maguire and Albright, 2005.

115 Christensen-Szalaski and Bushyhead, 1981.

116 Kardes, 2006.

117 Einhorn and Hogarth, 1978.

118 Poynard et al., 2002; see also Arbesman, 2012.

119 Poynard et al., 2002.

120 Arbesman, 2012.

121 Rennie and Chalmers, 2009.

122 Ioannidis, 2005b.

123 See *Unreliable Research: Trouble at the Lab. The Economist*, Saturday 19 October 2013. www.economist.com/news/briefing/ 21588057-scientists-think-science-self-correcting-alarming-degree-it-not-trouble for a very accessible account of the logic behind these scientific failures.

124 Ioannidis, 2005a.

125 Ioannidis, 2008, p. 645.

126 Kuhn, 1962.

127 Lakatos, 1976, p. 49; see also Priest and Thomason, 2007.

128 Lakatos, 1976, p. 49.

129 Adams, 1995.

130 Verran, 2002; Carr, 2004; Broks, 2006.

131 Agrawal, 1995; Jasanoff, 2006; Broks, 2006; Evans, 2008.

132 Collins and Evans, 2007.

133 Gregory et al., 2006.

4 DEALING WITH INDIVIDUAL EXPERTS

1 Burgman et al., 2011b.

2 Speirs-Bridge et al., 2010.

3 See Walley, 1991; van Frassen, 1984; McKaughan and Drake, 2012.

4 Beyth-Marom, Dekel, Gombo and Shaked, 1985.

5 While structurally similar, the 4-point format differs from existing methods for eliciting quantitative estimates of uncertainty (e.g. O'Neill et al., 2008; Murray et al., 2009; O'Leary et al., 2009; Rothlisberger et al., 2010), which typically involve the use of greater numbers of questions per parameter, and more statistically complex concepts. By asking participants to consider evidence that might support the bounds of their judgements, and to consider counter-factual reasoning, we encourage both individual and group estimates to improve. See Herzog and Hertwig, 2009.

6 Lichtenstein, Fischhoff and Phillips, 1982; Russo and Schoemaker, 1992; Soll and Klayman, 2004. See Speirs-Bridge et al., 2010; Klayman, Soll, Juslin and Winman, 2006. There may be at least two independent mechanisms in play, knowledge sampling (Soll and Klayman, 2004) and interval judgement (Juslin and Winman, 2006), Teigan and Jorgensen, 2005.

7 Morgan and Henrion (1990) also suggested asking first for extreme values for an uncertain quantity. That is, the analyst elicits the maximum and minimum 'credible' values, before asking for the best estimate, to help overcome overly narrow bounds. Then, they suggested that the assessor ask the respondent to think about scenarios that produce values outside the extremes.

8 Usually, we ask people to specify level of confidence between 50 per cent and 100 per cent. If their confidence is lower than 50%, it can mean the best guess is more likely to be outside the interval than inside it. However, some people may be more comfortable indicating bounds that enclose the 40th and 60th quantiles of a distribution, in which case they may wish to stipulate a confidence of less than 50 per cent.

9 907.

10 Quantitative estimates elicited using the 4-point estimation method may be normalised using linear extrapolation (Bedford and Cooke, 2001) to absolute lower (α_{abs}) and upper (β_{abs}) bounds within which 100 per cent of all estimates might be expected to fall such that

$$\alpha_{abs} = \gamma + (\beta - \gamma)(c/\rho)$$
$$\beta_{abs} = Y - (\gamma - \alpha)(c/\rho)$$

where c is the required possibility level (100 per cent) and ρ is the expert's stated confidence. These 100 per cent interval bounds may be used as the minimum and maximum values for triangular numbers, and the best guess (γ) is usually taken as the most likely value. The same approach, using $c = 80$ per cent, generates standardised 80 per cent intervals for experts to view and compare responses at the feedback stage of the elicitation. See, for example, McBride et al., 2012a; Galway, 2007.

11 Wintle, 2013.

12 Speirs-Bridge et al., 2010.

13 Lawrence, Goodwin, O'Connor and Onkal, 2006; Hora, 2007; James, Low Choy and Mengersen, 2010.

14 Morgan and Henrion (1990) also suggested asking first for extreme values for an uncertain quantity. That is, the analyst elicits the maximum and minimum 'credible' values, before asking for the best estimate, to help overcome overly narrow bounds. Then, they suggested that the assessor ask the respondent to think about scenarios that produce values outside the extremes.

15 Low Choy, O'Leary and Mengersen, 2009; O'Hagan, 2012.

16 Hoffman, Fischbeck, Krupnick and McWilliams, 2008.

17 The question and resolution information are derived from a real case study, albeit with different time frames, part of an IARPA supported experiment into the accuracy of geopolitical forecasting. See www.iarpa.gov/Programs/ia/ACE/ace.html.

18 Jaynes, 1976; Savage, 1972.

19 Morgan and Henrion, 1990.

20 de Finetti, 1974.

The objective is to elicit a judgement for a probability, p, that event E will occur. The reference lottery is in the form of a tree and the idea is to ask the expert to adjust the value of p to the point that they are indifferent to which lottery they could be involved in. The value for p that results from application of the reference lottery is taken to be the probability that the event will occur.

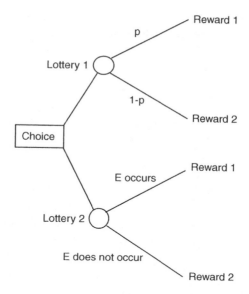

Reference lottery for the probability that event E will occur. The expert is asked to choose between Lottery 1 and Lottery 2. Usually, Reward 1 is less than Reward 2 when E is a low probability event. The value of p is adjusted until the person is indifferent between the choice of the two lotteries (de Finetti, 1974). To elicit preferences, Lottery 2 can be an outcome that happens for sure.

21 Dyer and Miles, 1976.

22 Coolen, 2004.

23 Walley (1991, 2000a,b) defined imprecise probabilities as a *gamble*. Subjective upper and lower probabilities based on buying and selling prices for gambles have comparable meanings (Walley and de Cooman, 2001). The probabilities $[p_{lower}, p_{upper}]$ embody a commitment to act in certain ways (a behavioural model; Walley and de Cooman, 2001). For example, E might be the amount of rain that will fall next week, regarded as a reward. It is rational to pay any price smaller than $\$X_B$ for the uncertain reward E. It is rational to sell the reward for any price higher than $\$X_S$. If the price is between $\$X_B$ and $\$X_S$, it may be reasonable to do nothing, to buy or to sell E. The buying and selling prices for risky investments offered by traders in financial markets are examples of such bounds (Walley, 2000a). Rather than ask for probabilities directly, it may

be easier to ask for the number of events that would arise from a larger set of possibilities. For example, hydrologist Mark Borsuk wanted expert information about the time between mixing events in an estuary. Rather than ask for the probabilities of different intervals, he asked, *'If you were to observe 100 vertical mixing events, how many do you think would be x days apart?'*.

24 Morgan and Henrion, 1990.

25 Dieckmann, Mauro and Slovic, 2010.

26 Vose, 1996; see also Ayyub, 2001.

27 After Wiggins, 1985 in Cooke, 1991.

28 After Cooke, 1991.

29 Mastrandrea et al., 2010.

30 See Burgman et al., 2000; Regan et al., 2001 for examples; and see Ayyub, 2001; Klir and Weirman, 1998; Walley and DeCooman, 2001 for methods.

31 Windschitl, 2002.

32 McBride et al., 2012a.

33 See Morgan and Henrion, 1990; Vose, 1996; Flander et al., 2012 for methods for eliciting probability distributions. Frequency formats are relatively robust to the inconsistencies of human perception (Gigerenzer, 2002). Eliciting dependencies reliably is difficult. In general, people have poor intuition unless dependencies are strong (i.e. close to −1 or +1; Morgan and Henrion, 1990). Cooke and Kraan (2000) developed a method that depends on a series of questions about conditional probabilities among pairs of variables of interest. Mechanistic understanding of dependencies and model disaggregation may also be useful (French, 2011). Instead of estimating an entire distribution, it may be sufficient to estimate the probability of a discrete event. For example, ocean storm damage is often represented as a function of the maximum wave height, and the chance of failure of a mining tailings pond may be viewed as the tail probability of the distribution of flood heights (Bier et al., 1999). Eliciting a realistic tail depends on the ability of the analyst to describe scenarios that result from correlated events, common failure modes, or the confluence of unusual occurrences from independent sources (Vose, 1996). When the mean and variance of a distribution are known with reasonable certainty, extreme value theory (Gumbel, 1958) can be used to estimate the probabilities of tails, even when the exact functional form of

the distribution is unknown. This approach may be unreliable if the physical mechanisms that generate events of different magnitudes are different (Bier et al., 1999).

34 Personal communication.

35 Gans and Palmer, 2004.

36 Cooke, 1991.

37 e.g. Cooke and Goossens, 2000; see Morgan and Henrion, 1990; Hoffrage et al., 2002; O'Hagan and Oakley, 2004; Lin and Bier, 2008. Appeals for more explicit testing have also appeared in legal academic reviews (Schum and Morris, 2007).

38 e.g. Cooke, 1991; Murphy, 1993; see also Fischhoff et al., 1982; Murphy and Winkler, 1977; Hora, 1992. A complete review of these techniques and their implications is beyond the scope of this review. Scoring rules measure the difference between actual outcomes and judgements. A scoring rule is 'proper' if it rewards assessors for giving their true opinion (Morgan and Henrion, 1990; Cooke, 1991). The 'reward' is a score, fed back to the expert. The efficacy of such rewards is questionable, especially when experts advocate a value-laden position.

39 Cooke, 1991; Cooke and Goossens, 2000.

40 Wright, Bolger and Rowe, 2002.

41 Cooke and Goossens, 2000.

42 e.g. Kadane et al., 1980; Cooke, 1991; Chaloner et al., 1993; Garthwaite et al., 2005.

43 Pidgeon et al., 2008.

44 McBride et al., 2012b.

45 Cooke and Goossens, 2000.

46 Dawes, 1994.

47 French, 2011, 2012.

48 Bedford, Quigley and Walls, 2006.

49 Redrawn from Carlon et al., 2001.

50 After Hart et al. in prep.

51 After Borsuk et al., 2003; Stow and Borsuk, 2003.

52 *Ibid.*

53 Shipley, 2000. In general, there are $N!/(4^{2!(N-2)!})$ combinations of N variables.

54 See Korb, 2003.

55 Freudenburg, 1992; MacGregor, 2001.

56 Bier et al., 1999.

57 Goodwin and Wright, 2010.

58 French, 2011.

59 Vose, 1996; Bier et al., 1999.

60 Hora, 2007.

61 After Cooke, 1991.

62 *Ibid.*

63 Donelan, Wingfield, Crowder and Wilcox, 2010.

64 Bier et al., 1999.

65 Benda et al., 2002.

66 Hilborn and Mangel, 1997.

5 THE WISDOM OF CROWDS REVISITED

1 Aristotle, p. 108.

2 Galton, 1907.

3 Gordon, 1924.

4 Galton, 1907.

5 Kosinski et al., 2012. The scores were based on a nonverbal multiple-choice general intelligence test. The IQ scale characteristic is standardised on a representative population to follow a normal distribution with an average score of 100 and standard deviation of 15.

6 Winkler and Poses, 1993; Surowiecki, 2004; Woolley et al., 2010; Lyle, 2008; Armstrong, 2001, pp. 417–439.

7 Surowiecki, 2004.

8 *Predicting the Facebook IPO: the crowd gets it wrong,* V. Miettinen, June 2012, Microtask, accessed March 9, 2013, http://blog.microtask.com/2012/06/predicting-the-facebook-ipo-the-crowd-gets-it-wrong/.

9 Kosinski et al., 2012.

10 *Ibid.*

11 Gowers and Nielsen, 2009.

12 Cranshaw and Kittur, 2011.

13 Jacob, 2011.

14 Khatib et al., 2011.

15 Hong and Page, 2004; Stirling, 2007; Woolley et al., 2010; Hoogendoorn et al., 2011.

16 For discussion, see Krinitzsky, 1993; Bottom et al., 2002; Tetlock, 2005.

17 e.g. Kerr, 1996.

18 Armstrong, 2001, pp. 417–439.

19 Janis, 1982; Lehrer, 2012.

20 *Report on the U.S. Intelligence Community's Prewar Intelligence Assessments on Iraq*, United States Senate Select Committee on Intelligence. July 2004, accessed March 9, 2013, http://web.mit .edu/simsong/www/iraqreport2-textunder.pdf. See also Tetlock and Mellers, 2011.

21 *Report on the U.S. Intelligence Community's Prewar Intelligence Assessments on Iraq*, United States Senate Select Committee on Intelligence, pp. 18, 26. July 2004, accessed March 9, 2013, http://web.mit.edu/simsong/www/iraqreport2-textunder.pdf.

22 Heuer Jr, 2005.

23 *Ibid.*

24 Cooke, 1991; Tetlock and Mellers, 2011; French, 2011.

25 See Webler et al., 1991; Cooke, 1991; Burgman, 2005.

26 Cooke, 1991; Ayyub, 2001; Kahn and Wiener, 1967.

27 See also Cooke and Goossens' (2000) expert procedures guide.

28 Rowe and Wright, 2001.

29 See Cooke, 1991; Vose, 1996; Mellers et al., 2015.

30 Bolger, Stranieri, Wright and Yearwood, 2011.

31 See Regan et al. (2002); Schultz-Hardt et al. (2006); and Schultze, Mojzisch and Schulz-Hardt (2012) for various aspects on these topics.

32 Franklin et al., 2008.

33 Nemeth et al., 2001; Bolger et al., 2011.

34 Gustafson, Shukla, Delbecq and Walster, 1973.

35 Graefe and Armstrong, 2011.

36 Wintle et al., 2012.

37 e.g. Elmer, Seifert, Kreibich and Thieke, 2010; MacMillan and Marshall, 2006.

38 Marcot et al., 2012.

39 e.g. MacMillan and Marshall, 2006.

40 McBride et al., 2012a.

41 See Cooke, 1991; Ayyub, 2001; see modifcations suggested by Vose, 1996.

42 Chamberlin, 1890.

43 The nominal group method begins in the same way as the Delphi method. Each participant considers the question and forms a private judgement, or outlines a solution to a problem. The facilitator collates

responses, amalgamates equivalent judgements and creates a list of options. Participants are shown the list and rank the options from most to least preferred. The ranks are equivalent to a score. If a participant ranks option A first, it scores maximum points. If there are three options and a participant scores option C second and option B third, their scores will be A:3, B:1, C:2. Each participant scores the options independently. The scores for each option are added and the option with the highest score is selected. This scoring approach is equivalent to voting (specifically, a voting method called the Borda count). Like the Delphi method, the facilitator may elect to encourage participants to talk after they have made their initial assessment, to reconcile the meanings of the questions and share the reasons for their choices.

44 Chen and Plott, 2002.

45 After www.ipredict.co.nz; date accessed: August 6, 2014.

46 Hanson, 2006.

47 Chen and Plott, 2002.

48 *When the crowd isn't wise*, D. Leonhardt, *The New York Times Sunday Review*, July, 2012, accessed March 9, 2013, www.nytimes .com/2012/07/08/sunday-review/when-the-crowd-isnt-wise.html?_r=0; *Leonhardt blows it*, R. Hanson, Overcoming bias, July 2012, accessed March 9, 2013, www.overcomingbias.com/2012/07/leonhardt-blows-it .html.

49 Graefe and Armstrong, 2011.

50 Wintle et al., 2012.

51 Stasser and Titus, 1985; Libby, Trotman and Zimmer, 1987; Kerr and Tindale, 2004; Stirling, 2007.

52 Perspectives are often inseparable from social identities, and even in open and critical settings there are limits to people's ability to transcend their background and free themselves of their biases and prejudice…the absence of women and ethnic minorities from a scientific consensus, even if not intentional, constitutes a serious cognitive flaw, which reduces the community's critical resources. (Miller, 2013).

53 Stern and Fineberg (1996) outline objective methods for stratifying and selecting stakeholder participants.

54 FAO/WHO, 2001.

55 Clemen and Winkler, 1999.

56 For full details, see Stewart and Melchers, 1997.

57 After US Nuclear Regulatory Commission, 1975, in Stewart and Melchers, 1997, p. 87.

58 See the reviews by Wallsten, Budescu, Erev and Diederich (1997); Clemen and Winkler (1999).

59 Clemen and Winkler, 1999.

60 Valverde (2001) suggested a framework to achieve consensus expert opinion that has its foundations in an approach developed by Kaplan (1992). It involves diagnosing sources of disagreement and finding ways to resolve them. Valverde used the typology for arguments invented by Toulmin (1958) that recognises five basic elements:

- Claim: an assertion or proposition, usually the end result of an argument, but neither necessarily certain or true.
- Data: information content of an argument, including physical evidence, observations and experimental values.
- Warrant: the causal laws, inference mechanisms, models or rules that link the data to the claim.
- Backing: background assumptions or foundations that support the warrant, including axioms, theory and formal principles.
- Rebuttal: the conditions under which and the reasons why the claim does not necessarily hold, and which may apply to the warrant or the claim.

61 Punt and Hilborn, 1997.

62 Valverde (2001) created a second taxonomy to diagnose sources of disagreement:

- Semantic disagreement: experts misunderstand the meanings of words.
- Preference disagreement: experts have different preferences for methods and standards used to evaluate claims.
- Alternative disagreement: usually management options are offered that serve to frame a problem, but experts differ in their views about the admissible set of policy options.
- Information disagreement: experts differ in their views on measurements, the validity of experiments, the methods used to obtain observations, or the rules of inference.
- Epistemic disagreement: experts adhere to different scientific theories, professional conventions or ethical positions.

63 van Gelder, 2013.

64 Engelhardt and Caplan, 1986.

65 Clemen and Winkler, 1999.

66 Miller, 2013.

67 Dawid et al., 1995.

68 Approaches such as evidence theory (see Sentz and Ferson, 2002; Ferson et al., 2003; Klir and Weirman, 1998; Zadeh, 1986) have been developed to cope with non-probabilistic uncertainty. When probabilities are themselves uncertain, the analyst may use bounds on probabilities (Walley, 1991).

69 See Cooke, 1991; Vose, 1996; Valverde, 2001; French, 2011.

$$P_{1...n}(A) = \frac{1}{n}\sum w_i p_i(A)$$

where w_i are non-negative weights, p_i is the subjective belief of expert I associated with the value of A, and n is the number of experts. This is sometimes termed mixing or averaging. Cooke (1991) generalised this expression to include a range of options from arithmetic averaging to logarithmic weights based of the products of the probabilities given by the experts,

$$p(A) = k\prod_{i=1}^{n} p_i(A)^{w_i}$$

k is a normalisation value to ensure probabilities add to 1. However, there is no underlying general theory that can justify the selection of the weights or the function that combines them (Clemen and Winkler, 1999) beyond the empirical strategies developed by Cooke (1991).

70 Gigone and Hastie, 1997; Clemen and Winkler, 1999; Armstrong, 2001, pp. 417–439. When the data are naturally bounded by zero (such as counts, rainfall data), and are right-skewed, then they may have many properties that are often considered to be typical of a log-normal distribution. Spiegelhalter (pers. comm.) has found the geometric mean of a set of expert judgements to be effective in such situations. It follows from people tending to make relative rather than absolute errors.

71 Peachy, Spiegelhalter and Marteau, 2013.

72 Spiegelhalter, Harris and Franklin, 1994.

73 Cooke, 1991; Goossens and Cooke, 2001.

74 Cooke, 1991; see also Cooke and Goossens, 2000; Goossens and Cooke, 2001; Keeney and von Winterfeldt, 1991.

75 The procedures guide for expert judgement. The procedure has 15 steps:

1. Definition of case structure: This is achieved by creating a document that specifies all the issues to be considered during the expert judgement exercise. It provides information on where the results of the exercise will be used, and outlines the physical phenomena and models for which expert assessment is required.

2. Identification of target variables: A procedure is used to select variables for expert elicitation, to limit them to a manageable number. Variables are included if they are important and if historical data are insufficient or unavailable.

3. Identification of query variables: If target variables are not appropriate for direct elicitation, surrogate 'query' variables are constructed that ask for observable quantities, using questions formulated in a manner consistent with the experts' knowledge base.

4. Identification of performance variables: Performance (seed) variables are supported with experimental evidence that is unknown to the experts, but known to the analyst, usually from within or closely associated with the domain of the enquiry at hand.

5. Identification of experts: As large a list as possible is compiled of people whose past or present field contains the subject in question and who are regarded by others as being knowledgeable about the subject.

6. Selection of experts: A subset is selected by a committee based on reputation, experimental experience, publication record, familiarity with uncertainty concepts, diversity of background, awards, balance of views, interest in the project and availability.

7. Definition of elicitation format: A document is created that gives the questions, provides explanations and the format for the assessments.

8. Dry run exercise: Two experienced people review the case structure and elicitation format documents, commenting on ambiguities and completeness.

9. Expert training: Experts are trained to provide judgements of uncertain variables in terms of quantiles for cumulative distributions, anchoring their judgements to familiar landmarks such as the 5th, 50th and 95th quantiles.

10. Expert elicitation session: Each expert is interviewed individually by an analyst experienced in probability together with a substantive expert with relevant experience. Typically, they are asked to provide subjective judgements for the query variables as quantiles of cumulative distributions.

11. Combination of expert assessments: Estimates are combined to give a single probability distribution for each variable. Experts may be weighted equally, or by assigning weights reflecting performance on seed questions.

12. Robustness and discrepancy analysis: Robustness may be calculated for experts by removing their opinions from the data set, one at a time, and recalculating the combined functions. Large information loss suggests that the results may not be replicated if another study was done with different experts. A similar evaluation may be conducted for seed variables. Discrepancy analysis identifies the items on which the experts differ most.

13. Feedback: Each expert is provided their assessment, an informativeness score, weights given to their opinion, and passages from the final report in which their name is used.

14. Post-processing analysis: Aggregated results may be adjusted to give appropriate distributions for the required input parameters.

15. Documentation: This involves the production of the formal report.

76 Cooke, 1991; French, 2012.

77 Kaplan (1992), for instance, outlined a method that uses some of the structured approach of Cooke (1991) together with some elements of consensus and negotiation described by Valverde (2001). It is similar to the structured expert judgement procedure because it assumes a real valued parameter that experts try to estimate in a structured elicitation process. It is similar to the framework developed by Valverde (2001) in insisting that experts document and communicate the evidence they bring to any argument, and that they be prepared to negotiate to a group consensus. Horst et al. (1998) used experts to estimate the chances that new diseases would arrive in the Netherlands on imported foods. They were concerned about six viral diseases, including foot-and-mouth disease, swine fever, swine vesicular disease, Newcastle disease and avian influenza.

78 Abbas, 2009; Bedford and Cooke, 2001; Bier, 2004.

79 Spiegelhalter, Harris and Franklin, 1994.

80 Clemen and Winkler, 1999; O'Hagan et al., 2006; Albert et al., 2012. Many of these studies and their associated discussions provide interesting ideas on how to generate statistical distributions from expert judgements.

81 MacDonald, Small and Norgan, 2008.

82 *Ibid.*

6 TIPS TO GET THE BEST OUT OF EXPERTS

1 Simon, 1959; Lempert, Groves, Popper and Bankes, 2006; Ben-Haim, 2006.

2 Armstrong, 1980.

3 See also the excellent review by Morgan, 2014.

4 Hall, 2011.

5 *The L'Aquila verdict: a judgment not against science, but against a failure of science communication*, D. Ropeik, October, 2012, *Scientific American* Guest Blog, accessed March 9, 2013, http://blogs .scientificamerican.com/guest-blog/2012/10/22/the-laquila-verdict-a-judgment-not-against-science-but-against-a-failure-of-scie nce-communication/

6 Hall, 2011.

7 *The L'Aquila verdict: a judgment not against science, but against a failure of science communication*, D. Ropeik, October, 2012, *Scientific American* Guest Blog, accessed March 9, 2013, http://blogs .scientificamerican.com/guest-blog/2012/10/22/the-laquila-verdict-a-judgment-not-against-science-but-against-a-failure-of-scie nce-communication/

8 Kloprogge, van der Sluijs and Wardekker, 2007; Caponecchia, 2009.

9 Gregory et al., 2012.

10 Finkel, 1996; Perhac, 1998; Veatch, 1991.

11 Perhac, 1998.

12 Adams, 1995; O'Brien, 2000; Fischer, 2000. See the review by Spruijt, 2014.

13 Walton, 1997; Fischer, 2000.

14 O'Brien, 2000.

15 Poff et al., 2003.

16 Jasanoff, 2007.

References

Abbas, A. E. 2009. A Kullback-Leibler view of linear and log-linear pools. *Decision Analysis* 6, 25–37.

Adams, J. 1995. *Risk.* UCL Press, London.

Agrawal, A. 1995. Indigenous and scientific knowledge: some critical comments. *Indigenous Knowledge and Development Monitor* 3, 3–6.

Albert, I., Donnet, S., Guihenneuc-Jouyaux, C., Low-Choy, S., Mengersen, K. and Rousseau, J. 2012. Combining expert opinions in prior elicitation. *Bayesian Analysis* 7, 503–532.

Aldy, J. E. and Viscusi, W. K. 2007. Age differences in the value of statistical life: revealed preference evidence. *Review of Environmental Economics and Policy* 1, 241–260.

ALRC. 1985. *Evidence.* Australian Law Reform Commission Report 26. Volume 1. Australian Government Publishing Service, Canberra.

ALRC. 2000. *Managing justice: a review of the Federal Civil Justice system.* Australian Law Reform Commission Report 89. Australian Government Publishing Service, Canberra.

Anderson, J. L. 1998. Embracing uncertainty: the interface of Bayesian statistics and cognitive psychology. *Conservation Ecology* 2, 2.

Arbesman, S. 2012. *The half-life of facts. Why everything we know has an expiration date.* Penguin, New York.

Aristotle. *Politics.* Volume 3. Translated by Ernest Barker, 1995. Oxford World's Classics.

Armstrong, J. S. 1980. The seer-sucker theory: the value of experts in forecasting. *Technology Review* 82, 16–24.

Armstrong, J. S. 2001. *Principles of forecasting: a handbook for researchers and practitioners.* Kluwer Academic Publishers, Dordrecht.

Armstrong, J. S. 2006. Findings from evidence-based forecasting: methods for reducing forecast error. *International Journal of Forecasting* 22, 583–598.

Ashton, R. 2000. A review and analysis of research on the test–retest reliability of professional judgment. *Journal of Behavioral Decision Making* 13, 277–294.

Aspinall, W. 2010. A route to more tractable expert advice. *Nature* 463, 294–295.

Athanasopoulos, G. and Hyndman, R. J. 2011. The value of feedback in forecasting competitions. *International Journal of Forecasting* 27, 845–849.

Ayyub, B. M. 2001. *Elicitation of expert opinions for uncertainty and risks*. CRC Press, Boca Raton, Florida.

Ball, D., Maggs, D. and Barrett, M. 2009. *Judges, courts, the legal profession and public risk*. Risk and Regulation Advisory Council, UK.

Bar-Hillel, M. 1980. The base-rate fallacy in probability judgments. *Acta Psychologica* 44, 211–233.

Barber, B. M. and Odean, T. 2001. Boys will be boys: Gender, overconfidence, and common stock investment. *Quarterly Journal of Economics* 116, 261–292.

Barley, S. R. and Kunda G. 2006. Contracting: a new form of professional practice. *Academy of Management Perspectives* 20, 45–66.

Beck, U. 1992. *Risk society: towards a new modernity*. Sage Publications, London.

Bedford, T. and Cooke, R. 2001. *Probabilistic risk analysis: foundations and methods*. Cambridge University Press.

Bedford, T., Quigley, J. and Walls, L. 2006. Expert elicitation for reliable system design. *Statistical Science* 21, 428–450.

Beissinger, S. R. and Westphal, M. I. 1998. On the use of demographic models of population viability in endangered species management. *Journal of Wildlife Management* 62, 821–841.

Benda, L. E., Poff, N. L., Tague, C., Palmer, M. A., Pizzuto, J., Cooper, S., Stanley, E. and Moglen, G. 2002. How to avoid train wrecks when using science in environmental problem solving. *Bioscience* 52, 1127–1136.

Ben-Haim, Y. 2006. *Information-gap decision theory: decisions under severe uncertainty*. Academic Press, San Diego.

Benson, P. G. and Nichols, M. L. 1982. An investigation of motivational bias in subjective predictive probability distributions. *Decision Sciences* 13, 225–239.

Bernard, H. B. 1988. *Research methods in cultural anthropology*. Sage Publications, London.

Berner, E. S. and Graber, M. L. 2008. Overconfidence as a cause of diagnostic error in medicine. *American Journal of Medicine* 121, S2–S23.

Bernstein, P. L. 1996. *Against the Gods: the remarkable story of risk*. Wiley, New York.

Beyth-Marom, R., Dekel, S., Gombo, R. and Shaked, M. 1985. *An elementary approach to thinking under uncertainty*. Lawrence Erlbaum Associates, Hillside, New Jersey.

Bian, W.-Q. and Keller, L. R. 1999a. Chinese and Americans agree on what is fair, but disagree on what is best in societal decisions affecting health and safety risks. *Risk Analysis* 19, 439–452.

Bian, W.-Q. and Keller, L. R. 1999b. Patterns of fairness judgments in North America and the People's Republic of China. *Journal of Consumer Psychology* 8, 301–320.

Bier, V. 2004. Implications of the research on expert overconfidence and dependence. *Reliability Engineering and System Safety* 85, 321–329.

Bier, V. M., Haimes, Y. Y., Lambert, J. H., Matalas, N. C. and Zimmerman, R. 1999. A survey of approaches for assessing and managing the risk of extremes. *Risk Analysis* 19, 83–94.

Bolger, F., Stranieri, A., Wright, G. and Yearwood, J. 2011. Does the Delphi process lead to increased accuracy in group-based judgmental forecasts or does it simply induce consensus amongst judgmental forecasters? *Technological Forecasting and Social Change* 78, 1671–1680.

Borsuk, M. E., Stow, C. A. and Reckhow, K. H. 2003. An integrated approach to TMDL development for the Neuse River Estuary using a Bayesian probability network model (Neu-BERN). *Journal of Water Resources Planning and Management* 129, 271–282.

Bottom, W., Lakha, K. and Miller, G. J. 2002. Propagation of individual bias through group judgment: error in the treatment of asymmetrically informative signals. *Journal of Risk and Uncertainty* 25, 147–163.

Brier, G. W. 1950. Verification of forecasts expressed in terms of probability. *Monthly Weather Review* 78, 1–3.

Broks, P. 2006. *Understanding popular science.* Open University Press, Maidenhead, England.

Brooks, M. 2007. Can you believe the weather? *New Scientist* issue 2588, 27 January 2007, 32–35.

Burgman, M. A. 2005. *Risks and decisions for conservation and environmental management.* Cambridge University Press.

Burgman, M. A., Ferson, S. and Akçakaya, H. R. 1993. *Risk assessment in conservation biology.* Chapman and Hall, London.

Burgman, M. A., Maslin, B. R., Andrewartha, D., Keatley, M. R., Boek, C. and McCarthy, M. 2000. Inferring threat from scientific collections: power tests and application to Western Australian Acacia species. In S. Ferson and M. A. Burgman, editors. *Quantitative methods for conservation biology.* Springer-Verlag, New York.

Burgman, M. A., McBride, M., Ashton, R., Speirs-Bridge, A., Flander, L., Wintle, B., Fidler, F., Rumpff, L. and Twardy, C. 2011a. Expert status and performance. *PLoS ONE* 6, e22998.

Burgman, M.A., Carr, A., Godden, L., Gregory, R., McBride, M., Flander, L. and Maguire. L. 2011b. Redefining expertise and improving ecological judgement. *Conservation Letters* 4, 81–87.

Camerer, C. F. and Johnson, E. J. 1991. The process-performance paradox in expert judgment: how can experts know so much and predict so badly? In K. A. Ericsson and J. Smith, editors. *Towards a general theory of expertise: prospects and limits*. Cambridge University Press, New York.

Campbell, L. M. 2002. Science and sustainable use: views of marine turtle conservation experts. *Ecological Applications* 12, 1229–1246.

Capen, E. C. 1976. The difficulty of assessing uncertainty. *Journal of Petroleum Technology* 28, 843–850.

Caponecchia, C. 2009. Strategies to improve the communication of probability information in risk analyses. *International Journal of Risk Assessment and Management* 12, 380–395.

Carlon, C., Critto, A., Marcomini, A. and Nathanail, P. 2001. Risk based characterization of contaminated industrial site using multivariate and geostatistical tools. *Environmental Pollution* 111, 417–427.

Carpenter, S. R., Brock, W. A. and Hanson, P. C. 1999. *Ecological and social dynamics in simple models of ecosystem management.* Social Systems Research Institute, University of Wisconsin.

Carr, A. J. L. 2004. Why do we all need community science? *Society and Natural Resources* 17, 1–9.

Chaloner, K., Church, T., Louis, T. A. and Matts, J. P. 1993. Graphical elicitation of a prior distribution for a clinical trial. *The Statistician* 42, 341–353.

Chamberlin, T. C. 1890. The method of multiple working hypotheses. Reprinted in *Science* 148, 754–759.

Chatterjee, S. K. 2003. *Statistical thought: a perspective and history*. Oxford University Press.

Chen, K.-Y. and Plott, C. R. 2002. Information aggregation mechanisms: concepts, design and implementation for a sales forecasting problem. *Social Science Working Paper 1131*, California Institute of Technology.

Chesson, P. 1978. Predator–prey theory and variability. *Annual Review of Ecology and Systematics* 9, 323–347.

Chi, M. T. H. 2006. Two approaches to the study of experts' characteristics. In K. A. Ericsson, N. Charness, P. J. Feltovitch and R. R. Hoffman, editors. *The Cambridge handbook of expertise and expert performance*. Cambridge University Press.

Christensen-Szalanski, J. and Bushyhead, J. 1981. Physicians use of probabilistic information in a real clinical setting. *Journal of Experimental Psychology: Human Perception and Performance* 7, 928–935.

Clemen, R. T. and Winkler, R. L. 1999. Combining probability distributions from experts in risk analysis. *Risk Analysis* 19, 187–203.

Cocozza, J. J. and Steadman, H. J. 1978. Prediction in psychiatry: an example of misplaced confidence in experts. *Social Problems* 25, 265–276.

Collins, H. M. and Evans R. 2007. *Rethinking expertise.* University of Chicago Press.

Colyvan, M. 2001. Is probability the only coherent approach to uncertainty? *Risk Analysis* 28, 645–652.

Cooke, R. M. 1991. *Experts in uncertainty: opinion and subjective probability in science.* Oxford University Press.

Cooke, R. M., El Saadany, S. and Xinzheng Huang, X. 2008. On the performance of social network and likelihood based expert weighting schemes. *Reliability Engineering and System Safety*, Special Issue 93, 745–756.

Cooke, R. M. and Goossens, L. H. J. 2000. Procedures guide for structured expert judgement in accident consequence modelling. *Radiation Protection and Dosimetry* 90, 303–309.

Cooke, R. M. and Kraan, B. 2000. Processing expert judgements in accident consequence modelling. *Radiation Protection Dosimetry* 90, 311–315.

Coolen, F. P. A. 2004. On the use of imprecise probabilities in reliability. *Quality and Reliability Engineering International* 20, 193–202.

Cranshaw, J. and Kittur, A. 2011. The Polymath Projects: lessons from an experiment in large-scale online collaboration in mathematics. In *Proceedings of the SIGCHI Conference on Human Factors in Computing Systems*, 1865–1874. ACM.

Crawford-Brown, D. J. 1999. *Risk-based environmental decisions: method and culture.* Kluwer Academic Publishers, Boston.

Davis, D. A., Mazmanian, P. E., Fordis, M., Van, H. R., Thorpe, K. E., Perrier, L. 2006. Accuracy of physician self-assessment compared with observed measures of competence: a systematic review. *Journal of the American Medical Association* 296, 1094–1102.

Dawes, R. M. 1979. The robust beauty of improper linear models in decision making. *American Psychologist* 34, 571–582.

Dawes, R. M. 1994. *House of cards: psychology and psychotherapy built on myth.* Simon and Schuster, New York.

Dawid, A. P., DeGroot, M. H., Mortera, J., Cooke, R., French, S., Genest, C., Schervish, J., Lindley, D. V., McConway, K. J. and Winkler, R. L. 1995. Coherent combination of experts' opinions. *Test* 4, 263–313.

de Finetti, B. 1974. *Theory of probability.* Wiley, New York.

Deffenbacher, K. A. 1980. Eyewitness accuracy and confidence. *Law and Human Behavior* 4, 243–260.

Denning, D., Johnson, K., Ehrlinger, J. and Kruger, J. 2003. Why people fail to recognize their own incompetence. *Current Directions in Psychological Science* 12, 83–87.

Dieckmann, N. F., Mauro, R. and Slovic, P. 2010. The effects of presenting imprecise probabilities in intelligence forecasts. *Risk Analysis* 30, 987–1001.

Dommelen, A. V. 1999. *Hazard identification of agricultural biotechnology: finding relevant questions.* International Books, Utrecht.

Donelan, C. J., Wingfield, D. K., Crowder, L. B. and Wilcox, C. 2010. Using expert opinion surveys to rank threats to endangered species: a case study with sea turtles. *Conservation Biology* 24, 1586–1595.

Dror, I. E., Peron, A. E., Hind, S. L. and Charlton, D. 2005. When emotions get the better of us: the effect of contextual top-down processing on matching fingerprints. *Applied Cognitive Psychology* 19, 799–809.

Dror, I. E. and Rosenthal, R. 2008. Meta-analytically quantifying the reliability and biasability of fingerprint experts' decision making. *Journal of Forensic Sciences* 53, 900–903.

Dyer, J. S. and Miles, R. F. 1976. An actual application of collective choice theory to the selection of trajectories for the Mariner Jupiter/Saturn 1977 project. *Operations Research* 24, 220–244.

Einhorn, H. J. and Hogarth, R. M. 1978. Confidence in judgment: persistence of the illusion of validity. *Psychological Review* 85, 395–416.

Elmer, F., Seifert, I., Kreibich, H. and Thieke, A. H. 2010. A Delphi method expert survey to derive standards for flood damage data collection. *Risk Analysis* 30, 107–124.

Elstein, A. S. 1995. Clinical reasoning in medicine. In: J. J. M. Higgs, editor. *Clinical Reasoning in the Health Professions.* Butterworth-Heinemann Limited, Oxford, England.

Engelhardt, H. and Caplan, H. 1986. Patterns of controversy and closure: the interplay of knowledge, values, and political forces. In H. Engelhardt and H. Caplan, editors. *Scientific controversies: case studies in the resolution and closure of disputes in science and technology.* Cambridge University Press, New York.

Engelmann, J. B., Capra, C. M., Noussair, C. and Berns, G. S. 2009. Expert financial advice neurobiologically "offloads" financial decision-making under risk. *PLoS ONE* 4, e4957.

Englich, B. and Soder, K. 2009. Moody experts – how mood and expertise influence judgmental anchoring. *Judgment and Decision Making* 4, 41–50.

Ericsson, K. A., Charness, N., Feltovich, P. J. and Hoffman, R. R., editors. 2006. *The Cambridge Handbook of Expertise and Expert Performance.* Cambridge University Press, New York.

European Food Safety Authority 2011. *Guidance on expert knowledge elicitation in food and feed safety risk assessment.* European Food Safety Authority (EFSA), Parma, Italy.

Evans, J. St. B. T. 2008. Dual-processing accounts of reasoning, judgment, and social cognition. *Annual Review of Psychology* 59, 255–278.

Evatts, J., Mieg, H. A. and Felt, U. 2006. Professionalization, scientific expertise, and elitism: a sociological perspective. In K. A. Ericsson, N. Charness, P. J. Feltovitch and R. R. Hoffman, editors. *The Cambridge handbook of expertise and expert performance.* Cambridge University Press.

Ezrahi, Y. 1990. *The descent of Icarus: science and the transformation of contemporary democracy.* Harvard University Press, Cambridge, Massachusetts.

Failing, L., Gregory, R. and Harstone, M. 2007. Integrating science and local knowledge in environmental risk management: a decision-focused approach. *Ecological Economics* 64, 47–70.

FAO / WHO. 2001. Call for experts for the Joint FAO / WHO risk assessment activities in the areas of *Campylobacter* in broilers and *Vibrio* in seafood. *Joint Expert Consultations on Risk Assessment of Microbiological Hazards in Food.* Food and Nutrition Division, Food and Agriculture Organization of the United Nations, Rome, Italy.

Ferson, S., Kreinovich, V., Ginzburg, L., Myers, D. and Sentz, K. 2003. Constructing probability boxes and Dempster–Shafer structures. *SAND Report, SAND2002-4015.* Sandia National Laboratories, Albuquerque, New Mexico.

Feynman, R. P. 1986. Appendix F – Personal observations on the reliability of the Shuttle. In *Hearing on the Space Shuttle Accident and the Rogers Commission Report.* Report of the Presidential Commission on the Space Shuttle Challenger Accident. U.S. Senate Committee on Commerce, Science and Transportation, Subcommittee on Science, Technology and Space, Washington, DC.

Figlewski, S. 1979. Subjective information and market efficiency in a betting market. *Journal of Political Economy* 87, 75–88.

Finkel, A. M. 1996. Comparing risks thoughtfully. *Risk,* 7, 325.

Fischer, F. 2000. *Citizens, experts, and the environment.* Duke University Press, Durham.

Fischhoff, B. 1994. Acceptable risk: a conceptual proposal. *Risk: Health, Safety and Environment* 1, 1–28.

Fischhoff, B. 1995. Risk perception and communication unplugged: twenty years of progress. *Risk Analysis* 15, 137–145.

Fischhoff, B., Slovic, P. and Lichtenstein, S. 1982. Lay foibles and expert fables in judgements about risk. *American Statistician* 36, 240–255.

Fisk, D. 1998. Environmental science and environmental law. *Journal of Environmental Law* 10, 3–8.

Flander, L., Dixon, W., McBride, M. and Burgman, M. 2012. Facilitated expert judgment of environmental risks: acquiring and analysing imprecise data. *International Journal of Risk Assessment and Management* 16, 199–212.

Forrester, Y. 2005. *The quality of expert judgment: an interdisciplinary investigation.* PhD Thesis. Department of Mechanical Engineering, University of Maryland. URL: http://hdl.handle.net/1903/3267.

Franklin, J., Sisson S. A., Burgman M. A. and Martin J. K. 2008. Evaluating extreme risks in invasion ecology: learning from banking compliance. *Diversity and Distributions* 14, 581–591.

Freckelton, I. 1995. The challenge of junk psychiatry, psychology and science: the evolving role of the forensic expert. In H. Selby, editor. *Tomorrow's law.* Federation Press, Sydney.

French, S. 2011. Aggregating expert judgement. *Revista De La Real Academia De Ciencias Exactas Fisicas Y Naturales Serie a-Matematicas* 105, 181–206.

French, S. 2012. Expert judgment, meta-analysis and participatory risk analysis. *Decision Analysis* 9, 119–127.

Freudenburg, W. R. 1992. Heuristics, biases, and the not-so-general publics: expertise and error in the assessment of risks. In S. Krimsky and D. Golding, editors. *Social theories of risk.* Praeger Publishing, Westport, Connecticut.

Freudenburg, W. R. 1996. Risky thinking: irrational fears about risk and society. *Annals of the American Academy of Political and Social Science* 545, 44–53.

Freudenburg, W. R. 1999. Tools for understanding the socioeconomic and political settings for environmental decision making. In V. H. Dale and M. R. English, editors. *Tools to aid environmental decision making.* Springer, New York.

Freudenburg, W. R., Coleman, C.-L., Gonzales, J. and Helgeland, C. 1996. Media coverage of hazard events: analyzing the assumptions. *Risk Analysis* 16, 31–42.

Fulero, S. M. 2009. System and estimator variables in eyewitness identification: a review (Chapter 3). In D. A. Krauss and J. D. Lieberman, editors. *Psychological expertise in court.* Ashgate Publishing, Farnham.

Galton, F. 1907. Vox populi. *Nature* 75, 450–451.

Galway, L. A. 2007. *Subjective probability distribution elicitation in cost risk analysis.* United States Airforce Report, RAND Corporation, Santa Monica.

Gans, J. and Palmer, A. 2004. *Australian principles of evidence.* Routledge Cavendish, Sydney.

Garthwaite, P. H., Kadane, J. B. and O'Hagan, A. 2005. Statistical methods for eliciting probability distributions. *Journal of the American Statistical Association* 100, 680–700.

Gigerenzer, G. 2002. *Calculated risks: how to know when numbers deceive you.* Simon and Schuster, New York.

Gigerenzer, G. 2007. *Gut feelings: the intelligence of the unconscious.* Viking Press, New York.

Gigerenzer, G., Hertwig, R. van den Broek, E., Fasolo, B. and Katsikopoulos, K. V. 2005. A 30% chance of rain tomorrow: How does the public understand probabilistic weather forecasts? *Risk Analysis* 25, 623–629.

Gigerenzer, G., Todd, P. M. and the ABC Research Group. 1999. *Simple heuristics that make us smart.* Oxford University Press, New York.

Gigone, D. and Hastie, R. 1997. Proper analysis of the accuracy of group judgments. *Psychological Bulletin* 121, 149–167.

Gilovich, T., Griffin, D., and Kahneman, D. 2002. *Heuristics and biases: the psychology of intuitive judgement.* Cambridge University Press.

Glimcher, P. W. and Rustichini, A. 2004. Neuroeconomics: the consilience of brain and decision. *Science* 306, 447–452.

Goldberg, L. R. 1965. Diagnosticians vs. diagnostic signs: the diagnosis of psychosis vs. neurosis from the MMPI. *Psychological Monographs* 79 (Whole No. 602).

Goldring, J. 2003. An introduction to statistical 'evidence'. *Australian Bar Review* 23, 239–262.

Good, I. J. 1959. Kinds of probability. *Science* 129, 443–447.

Goodwin, P. and Wright, G. 2010. The limits of forecasting methods in anticipating rare events. *Technological Forecasting and Social Change* 77, 355–368.

Goossens, L. H. J. and Cooke, R. M. 2001. Expert judgement elicitation in risk assessment. In I. Linkov and J. Palma-Oliveira, editors. *Assessment and management of environmental risks.* Kluwer Academic Publishers, Dordrecht.

Gordon, K. 1924. Group judgments in the field of lifted weights. *Journal of Experimental Psychology* 7, 398–400.

Gowers, T. and Nielsen, M. 2009. Massively collaborative mathematics: the Polymath Project. *Nature* 461, 879–881.

Graefe, A. and Armstrong, J. S. 2011. Comparing face-to-face meetings, nominal groups, Delphi and prediction markets on an estimation task. *International Journal of Forecasting* 27, 183–195.

Graham, J. D. and Hammitt, J. K. 1996. Refining the CRA framework. In J. C. Davies, editor. *Comparing environmental risks.* Resources for the Future, Washington, DC.

Gregory, R., Failing, L., Harstone, M., Long, G., McDaniels, T. and Ohlson, D. 2012. *Structured decision making.* Wiley-Blackwell, Chichester.

Gregory, R., Failing, L., Ohlson, D. and McDaniels, T. 2006. Some pitfalls of an overemphasis on science in environmental risk management decisions. *Journal of Risk Research* 9, 717–735.

Gregory, R., Lichtenstein, S. and MacGregor, D. 1993. The role of past states in determining reference points for policy decisions. *Organisational Behavior and Human Decision Processes* 55, 195–206.

Gregory, J. and Miller, S. 1998. *Science in public: communication, culture, and credibility*. Plenum Press, New York.

Green, K. C. and Armstrong, J. S. 2007. Global warming: forecasts by scientists versus scientific forecasting. *Energy and Environment* 18, 997–1021.

Grigg, A. E. 1958. Experience of clinicians and speech characteristics and statements of clients as variables in clinical judgment. *Journal of Consulting Psychology* 22, 315–319.

Grove, W. M. and Meehl, P. E. 1996. Comparative efficiency of informal (subjective, impressionistic) and formal (mechanical, algorithmic) prediction procedures: the clinical-statistical controversy. *Psychology, Public Policy, and Law* 2, 293–323.

Grove, W. M., Zald, D. H., Lebow, B. S., Snits, B. E. and Nelson, C. E. 2000. Clinical vs. mechanical prediction: a meta-analysis. *Psychological Assessment* 12, 19–30.

Gullet, W. 2000. The precautionary principle in Australia: policy, law and potential precautionary EIAs. *Risk: Health, Safety and Environment* 11, 93–124.

Gumbel, E. J. 1958. *Statistics of extremes*. Columbia University Press, New York.

Gustafson, D. H., Shukla, R. K., Delbecq, A. and Walster, G. W. 1973. A comparative study of differences in subjective likelihood estimates made by individuals, interacting groups, Delphi groups, and nominal groups. *Organizational Behavior and Human Performance* 9, 280–291.

Gustafson, L. L., Gustafson, D. H., Antognoli, M. C. and Remmenga, M. D. 2013. Integrating expert judgment in veterinary epidemiology: example guidance for disease freedom surveillance. *Preventive Veterinary Medicine* 109, 1–9.

Haack, S. 2001. An epistemologist in the bramble-bush: at the Supreme Court with Mr. Joiner. *Journal of Health Politics Policy and Law* 26, 217–248.

Hacking, I. 1975. *The emergence of probability: a philosophical study of early ideas about probability, induction and statistical inference*. Cambridge University Press, London.

Hall, S. S. 2011. Scientists on trial: at fault? *Nature* 477, 264–269.

Hanson, R. 2006. Designing real terrorism futures. *Public Choice* 128, 257–274.

Hart, A. 1986. *Knowledge acquisition for expert systems*. McGraw-Hill, New York.

Hayakawa, H., Fischbeck, P. S. and Fischhoff, B. 2000. Traffic accident statistics and risk perceptions in Japan and the United States. *Accident Analysis and Prevention* 32, 827–835.

Henrion, M. and Fischhoff, B. 1986. Assessing uncertainty in physical constants. *American Journal of Physics* 54, 791–798.

Hertwig, R. 2012. Tapping into the wisdom of the crowd – with confidence. *Science* 36, 303–304.

Herzog, S. M. and Hertwig, R. 2009. The wisdom of many in one mind. *Psychological Science* 20, 231–237.

Heuer Jr, R. J. 2005. Limits of intelligence analysis. *Orbis* 49, 75–94.

Hilborn, R. 1987. Living with uncertainty in resource management. *North American Journal of Fisheries Management* 7, 1–5.

Hilborn, R. and Mangel, M. 1997. *The ecological detective: confronting models with data.* Monographs in Population Biology 28. Princeton University Press, New Jersey.

Hilgartner, S. 1990. The dominant view of popularization: conceptual problems, political uses. *Social Studies of Science* 20, 519–539.

Hoffman, S., Fischbeck, P., Krupnick, A. and McWilliams, M. 2008. Informing risk-mitigation priorities using uncertainty measures derived from heterogeneous expert panels: a demonstration using foodborne pathogens. *Reliability Engineering and System Safety* 93, 687–698.

Hoffrage, U., Gigerenzer, G., Krauss, S. and Martignon, L. 2002. Representation facilitates reasoning: what natural frequencies are and what they are not. *Cognition* 84, 343–352.

Hogarth, R. M. 2001. *Educating intuition.* University of Chicago Press.

Hogarth, R. M. 2005. Deciding analytically or trusting your intuition? The advantages and disadvantages of analytic and intuitive thought. In T. Betsch and S. Haberstroh, editors. *The routines of decision making.* Lawrence Erlbaum Associates, Mahwah, New Jersey.

Hong, L. and Page, S. E. 2004. Groups of diverse problem solvers can outperform groups of high-ability problem solvers. *Proceedings of the National Academy of Sciences of the USA* 101, 16385–16389.

Hoogendoorn, S., Oosterbeek, H. and van Praag, M. 2011. The impact of gender diversity on the performance of business teams: evidence from a field experiment. *Tinbergen Institute Discussion Paper TI 2011–074/3.* Amsterdam School of Economics, University of Amsterdam.

Hora, S. C. 1992. Acquisition of expert judgment: examples from risk assessment. *Journal of Energy Engineering* 118, 136–148.

Hora, S. C. 2007. Eliciting probabilities from experts (Chapter 8). In W. Edwards, R. F. Miles and D. von Winterfeldt, editors. *Advances in decision analysis.* Cambridge University Press.

Horst, H. S., Dijkhuizen, A. A., Huirne, R. B. M. and De Leeuw, P. W. 1998. Introduction of contagious animal diseases into the Netherlands: elicitation of expert opinions. *Livestock Production Science* 53, 253–264.

Imwinkelried, E. J. 1993. The Daubert decision: Frye is dead: long live the Federal Rules of Evidence. *Trial* 29, 60–65.

Inayatullah, S. 2008. Six pillars: futures thinking for transforming. *Foresight* 10, 4–21.

International Monetary Fund. 2006. *Global Financial Stability Report*. World Economic and Financial Surveys, Washington.

Ioannidis, J. P. A. 2005a. Contradicted and initially stronger effects in highly cited clinical research. *Journal of the American Medical Association* 294, 218–228.

Ioannidis, J. P. A. 2005b. Why most published research findings are false. *PLoS Medicine* 2, e124.

Ioannidis, J. P. A. 2008. Why most discovered true associations are inflated. *Epidemiology*.19, 640–648.

Irwin, A. 2001. Constructing the scientific citizen: science and democracy in the biosciences. *Public Understanding of Science* 10, 1–18.

Jacob, A. 2011. How to build the global mathematics brain. *New Scientist* issue 2811, 4 May 2011, 10–11.

James, A., Low Choy, S. and Mengersen, K. 2010. Elicitator: an expert elicitation tool for regression in ecology. *Environmental Modelling and Software* 25, 129–145.

Jamtvedt, G., Young, J. M., Kristoffersen, D. T., O'Brien, M. A. and Oxman, A. D. 2006. Does telling people what they have been doing change what they do? A systematic review of the effects of audit and feedback. *Quality and Safety in Health Care* 15, 433–436.

Janis, I. L. *Groupthink: Psychological studies of policy decisions and fiascos.* Houghton Mifflin, Boston.

Jasanoff, S. 2006. Transparency in public science: purposes, reasons, limits. *Law and Contemporary Problems* 69, 21.

Jasanoff, S. 2007. Technologies of humility. *Nature* 450, 33.

Jaynes, E. T. 1976. Confidence intervals vs Bayesian intervals. In Harper and Hooker, editors. *Foundations of probability theory, statistical inference, and statistical theories of science.* Volume 2. D. Reidel Publishing, Dordrecht, Holland.

Johansson, P. O. 2002. On the definition and age-dependency of the value of a statistical life. *Journal of Risk and Uncertainty* 25, 251–263.

Johnson, D. D. P. and Fowler, J. H. 2011. The evolution of overconfidence. *Nature* 477, 317–320.

Johnson, J. E. V. and Bruce, A. C. 2001. Calibration of subjective probability judgments in a naturalistic setting. *Organizational Behavior and Human Decision Processes* 85, 265–290.

Johnson, R. H. and Blair, J. A. 1983. *Logical self-defense*, 2nd edition. McGraw-Hill Ryerson, Toronto.

Kadane, J. B., Dickeey, J., Winkler, R. L., Smith, W. and Peters, S. 1980. Interactive elicitation of opinion for a normal linear model. *Journal of the American Statistical Association* 75, 815–885.

Kahan, D. M. 2013. Ideology, motivated reasoning, and cognitive reflection. *Judgment and Decision Making* 8, 407–424.

Kahan, D. M. 2015. Climate science communication and the measurement problem. *Advances in Political Psychology* 36, 1–43.

Kahn, H. and Wiener, A. J. 1967. *The year 2000: a framework for speculation.* Macmillan, New York.

Kahneman, D. 2011. *Thinking, fast and slow.* Farrar, Straus, and Giroux, New York.

Kahneman, D. and Tversky, A. 1979. Prospect theory: an analysis of decision under risk. *Econometrica* 47, 263–291.

Kahneman, D. and Tversky, A. 1984. Choices, values, and frames. *American Psychologist* 39, 342–347.

Kaiser, J. 2002. Software glitch threw off mortality estimates. *Science* 296, 1945–1946.

Kalof, L., Dietz, T., Guagnano, G. and Stern, P. C. 2002. Race, gender and environmentalism: the atypical values and beliefs of white men. *Race, Gender and Class* 9, 1–19.

Kammen, D. M. and Hassenzahl, D. M. 1999. *Should we risk it? Exploring environmental, health, and technological problem solving.* Princeton University Press, New Jersey.

Kaplan, S. 1992. 'Expert opinion' versus 'expert opinions.' Another approach to the problem of eliciting/combining/using expert opinion in PRA. *Reliability Engineering and System Safety* 35, 61–72.

Kaplan, S. and Garrick, B. 1981. On the quantitative definition of risk. *Risk Analysis* 1, 11–27.

Kardes, F. R. 2006. When should consumers and managers trust their intuition? *Journal of Consumer Psychology* 16, 20–24.

Keeney, R. L. and von Winterfeldt, D. 1991. Eliciting probabilities from experts in complex technical problems. *IEEE Transactions on Engineering Management* 38, 191–201.

Kerr, R. 1996. A new way to ask the experts: rating radioactive waste risks. *Science* 274, 913–914.

Kerr, N. L. and Tindale, R. S. 2004. Group performance and decision making. *Annual Review of Psychology* 55, 623–655.

Khatib, F., DiMaio, F., Foldit Contenders Group, Foldit Void Crushers Group, Cooper, S., Kazmierczyk, M., Gilski, M., Krzywda, S., Zabranska, H., Pichova, I., Thompson, J., Popovic, Z., Jaskolski, M. and Baker, D. 2011. Crystal structure of a monomeric retroviral protease solved by protein folding game players. *Nature Structural and Molecular Biology* 18, 1175–1177.

Kirsch, E. W. 1995. Daubert v. Merrell Dow Pharmaceuticals: active judicial scrutiny of scientific evidence. *Food and Drug Law Journal* 50, 213–234.

Klayman, J., Soll, J. B., Juslin, P. and Winman, A. 2006. Subjective confidence and the sampling of knowledge. In K. Fiedler and P. Juslin, editors. *Information sampling and adaptive cognition.* Cambridge University Press, New York, pp. 153–182.

Klir, G. J. and Harmanec, D. 1997. Types and measures of uncertainty. In J. Kacprzyk, H. Nurmi and M. Fedrizzi, editors. *Consensus under fuzziness.* Kluwer Academic Publishers, Boston.

Klir, G. J. and Wierman, M. J. 1998. *Uncertainty-based information: elements of generalized information theory.* Physica-Verlag, Heidelberg.

Kloprogge, P., van der Sluijs, J. and Wardekker, A. 2007. *Uncertainty communication issues and good practice.* Copernicus Institute for Sustainable Development and Innovation. Report NWS-E-2007–199. Netherlands Environmental Assessment Agency, Utrecht.

Knol, A. B., Slottje, P., van der Sluijs, J. P. and Lebret, E. 2010. The use of expert elicitation in environmental health impact assessment: a seven step procedure. *Environmental Health* 9, 19.

Korb, K. B. and Nicholson, A. E. 2003. *Bayesian artificial intelligence.* CRC Press, Boca Raton, Florida.

Koriat, A. 2012. When two heads are better than one and why? *Science* 336, 360–362.

Kosinski, M., Bachrach, Y., Kasneci, G., Van-Gael, J. and Graepel, T. 2012. Crowd IQ: measuring the intelligence of crowdsourcing platforms. In *Proceedings of the 3rd Annual ACM Web Science Conference*, 151–160. ACM.

Krinitzsky, E. L. 1993. Earthquake probability in engineering – Part 1: the use and misuse of expert opinion. *Engineering Geology* 33, 257–288.

Kruger, J. and Dunning, D. 2009. Unskilled and unaware: how difficulties in recognizing one's own incompetence lead to inflated self-assessments. *Psychology* 1, 30–46.

Kuhn, T. S. 1962. *The structure of scientific revolutions.* University of Chicago Press.

Kunda, Z. 1990. The case for motivated reasoning. *Psychological Bulletin* 108, 480–498.

Lakatos, I. 1976. *Proofs and refutations*. Cambridge University Press.

Laughlin, P. R. and Ellis, A. L. 1986. Demonstrability and social combination processes on mathematical intellective tasks. *Journal of Experimental Social Psychology* 22, 177–189.

Lawrence, M., Goodwin, P., O'Connor, M. and Onkal, D. 2006. Judgmental forecasting: a review of progress over the last 25 years. *International Journal of Forecasting* 22, 493–518.

Lawson, J. D. 1900. *The law of expert and opinion evidence*, 2nd edition. T. H. Flood, Chicago.

Leadbeater, C. 2003. Amateurs: a 21st-century remake – social commentator Charles Leadbeater looks at the growing number of people in Britain taking a serious approach to pastime pursuits. *RSA Journal* 150, 22–25.

Lehrer, J. 2012. Groupthink: the brainstorming myth. *The New Yorker* 30, 12.

Lempert, R. J., Groves, D. G., Popper, S. W. and Bankes, S. C. 2006. A general, analytic method for generating robust strategies and narrative scenarios. *Management Science* 52, 514–528.

Lewandowsky, S. and Kirsner, K. 2000. Knowledge partitioning: context-dependent use of expertise. *Memory and Cognition* 28, 295–305.

Libby, R., Trotman, K. T. and Zimmer, I. 1987. Member variation, recognition of expertise, and group performance. *Journal of Applied Psychology* 72, 81–87.

Lichtenstein, S., Fischhoff, B. and Phillips, L. D. 1982. Calibration of probabilities: the state of the art to 1980. In D. Kahneman, P. Slovic and A. Tversky, editors. *Judgment under uncertainty: heuristics and biases*. Cambridge University Press, New York.

Lin, S.-W. and Bier, V. M. 2008. A study of expert overconfidence. *Reliability Engineering and System Safety* 93, 711–721.

Lipinski, M., Froelicher, V., Atwood, E., Tseitlin, A., Franklin, B., Osterberg, L., Do, D. and Myers, J. 2002. Comparison of treadmill scores with physician estimates of diagnosis and prognosis in patients with coronary artery disease. *American Heart Journal* 143, 650–658.

Low Choy, S., O'Leary, R. and Mengersen, K. 2009. Elicitation by design in ecology: using expert opinion to inform priors for Bayesian statistical models. *Ecology* 90, 265–277.

Luft, J. 1950. Implicit hypotheses and clinical predictions. *Journal of Abnormal and Social Psychology* 5, 756–760.

Lyle, J. A. 2008. Collective problem solving: are the many smarter than the few? *Durham Anthropology Journal* 15, 23–58.

MacDonald, J. A., Small, M. J. and Norgan, M. G. 2008. Explosion probability of unexploded ordnance: expert beliefs. *Risk Analysis* 28, 825–841.

MacGregor, D. G. 2001. Decomposition for judgmental forecasting and estimation. In S. Armstrong, editor. *Principles of forecasting: a handbook for researchers and practitioners*. Kluwer Academic Publishers, Boston.

MacMillan, D. C. and Marshall, K. 2006. The Delphi process – an expert-based approach to ecological modelling in data-poor environments. *Animal Conservation* 9, 11–19.

Maguire, L. and Albright, E. A. 2005. Can behavioral decision theory explain risk-averse fire management decisions? *Forest Ecology and Management* 211, 47–58.

Marcot, B. G., Allen, C. S., Morey, S., Shively, D. and White, R. 2012. An expert panel approach to assessing potential effects of bull trout reintroduction on federally listed salmonids in the Clackamas River, Oregon. *North American Journal of Fisheries Management* 32, 450–465.

Martin, A. D., Quinn, K. M., Ruger, T. W. and Kim, P. T. 2004. Competing approaches to predicting supreme court decision making. *Perspectives on Politics* 2, 761–767.

Mastrandrea, M. D., Field, C. B., Stocker, T. F., Edenhofer, O., Ebi, K. L., Frame, D. J., Held, H., Kriegler, E., Mach, K. J., Matschoss, P. R., Plattner, G.-K., Yohe, G. W. and Zwiers, F. W. 2010. *Guidance note for lead authors of the IPCC Fifth Assessment Report on consistent treatment of uncertainties*. Intergovernmental Panel on Climate Change.

McBride, M.F., Garnett, S.T., Szabo, J.K., Burbidge, A.H., Butchart, S.H.M., Christidis, L., Dutson, G., Ford, H.A., Loyn, R.H., Watson, D.M., and Burgman, M.A. 2012a. Structured elicitation of expert judgments for threatened species assessment: a case study on a continental scale using email. *Methods in Ecology and Evolution* 3, 906–920.

McBride, M.F., Fidler, F. and Burgman, M.A. 2012b. Evaluating the accuracy and calibration of expert predictions under uncertainty: predicting the outcomes of ecological research. *Diversity and Distributions* 18, 782–794.

McKaughan, D. J. and Drake, J. M. 2012. Representing vague opinion. *Principia* 16, 341–344.

Meehl, P. E. 1954. *Clinical versus statistical prediction: a theoretical analysis and review of the evidence*. University of Minnesota Press, Minneapolis.

Meehl, P. E. 1986. Causes and effects of my disturbing little book. *Journal of Personality Assessment* 50, 370–375.

Meer, E. 2001. *Using comparative risk to set pollution prevention priorities in New York State: a formula for inaction: a critical analysis of the New York*

State Department of Environmental Conservation Comparative Risk Project. A report from the New York State Assembly Legislative Commission on Toxic Substances and Hazardous Wastes. Assemblyman Steve Englebright, Chair. New York.

Mellers, B., Stone, E., Murray, T. et al. 2015. Identifying and cultivating superforecasters as a method of improving probabilistic predictions. *Perspectives on Psychological Science* 10, 267–281.

Meyer, M. A. and Booker, J. M. 1990. *Eliciting and analyzing expert judgment: a practical guide.* Office of Nuclear Regulatory Research, Division of Systems Research, US Nuclear Regulatory Commission, Washington, DC.

Miller, B. 2013. When is consensus knowledge based? Distinguishing shared knowledge from mere agreement. *Synthese*, 190, 1293–1316.

Moore, D. A. and Healy, P. J. 2008. The trouble with overconfidence. *Psychological Review* 115, 502–517.

Moore, D. A., Tanlu, L. and Bazerman, M. H. 2010. Conflict of interest and the intrusion of bias. *Judgment and Decision Making* 5, 37–53.

Morgan, M. G. 1993. Risk analysis and management. *Scientific American* 269, 32–42.

Morgan, M. G. 2014. Use (and abuse) of expert elicitation in support of decision making for public policy. *Proceedings of the National Academy of Sciences of the USA* 111, 7176–7184.

Morgan, M. G., Fischhoff, B., Lave, L. and Fischbeck, P. 1996. A proposal for ranking risk within Federal agencies. In J. C. Davies, editor. *Comparing environmental risks*. Resources for the Future, Washington, DC.

Morgan, M. G. and Henrion, M. 1990. *Uncertainty: a guide to dealing with uncertainty in quantitative risk and policy analysis.* Cambridge University Press.

Mullainathan, S., Noeth, M. and Schoar, A. 2012. *The market for financial advice: an audit study.* National Bureau of Economic Research Working Paper No. 17929. Cambridge, Massachusetts.

Munnichs, G. 2004. Whom to trust? Public concerns, late modern risks, and expert trustworthiness. *Journal of Agricultural and Environmental Ethics* 17, 113–130.

Murphy, A. H. 1993. What is a good forecast? An essay on the nature of goodness in weather forecasting. *American Meterological Society* 8, 281–293.

Murphy, A. H. and Winkler, R. L. 1977. Can weather forecasters formulate reliable probability forecasts of precipitation and temperature? *National Weather Digest* 2, 2–9.

Murphy, A. H. and Winkler, R. L. 1984. Probability forecasting in meteorology. *Journal of the American Statistical Association* 79, 489–500.

Murray, J. V., Goldizen, A. W., O'Leary, R. A., McAlpine, C. A., Possingham, H. P. and Choy, S. L. 2009. How useful is expert opinion for predicting the distribution of a species within and beyond the region of expertise? A case study using brush-tailed rockwallabies *Petrogale penicillata*. *Journal of Applied Ecology* 46, 842–851.

Neff, C. and Hueter, R. 2013. Science, policy, and the public discourse of shark 'attack': a proposal for reclassifying human-shark interactions. *Journal of Environmental Studies and Sciences* 3, 65–73.

Nemeth, C. J., Connell, J. B., Rogers, J. D. and Brown, K. S. 2001. Improving decision making by means of dissent. *Journal of Applied Social Psychology* 31, 48–58.

O'Brien, M. 2000. *Making better environmental decisions: an alternative to risk assessment*. MIT Press, Cambridge, Massachusetts.

O'Hagan, A. 2012. Probabilistic uncertainty specification: overview, elaboration techniques and their application to a mechanistic model of carbon flux. *Environmental Modelling and Software* 36, 35–48.

O'Hagan, A., Buck, C. E., Daneshkhah, A., Eiser, R., Garthwaite, P., Jenkinson, D., Oakley, J. and Rakow, T. 2006. *Uncertain judgements: eliciting experts' probabilities*. Wiley, Hoboken, New Jersey.

O'Hagan, A. and Oakley, J. E. 2004. Probability is perfect, but we can't elicit it perfectly. *Reliability Engineering and System Safety* 85, 239–248.

O'Leary, R. A., Low-Choy, S., Murray, J. V., Kynn, M., Denham, R., Martin, T. G. and Mengersen, K. 2009. Comparison of three expert elicitation methods for logistic regression on predicting the presence of the threatened brush-tailed rock-wallaby *Petrogale penicillata*. *Environmetrics* 20, 379–398.

O'Neill, S. J., Osborn, T. J., Hulme, M., Lorenzoni, I. and Watkinson, A. R. 2008. Using expert knowledge to assess uncertainties in future polar bear populations under climate change. *Journal of Applied Ecology* 45, 1649–1659.

Önkal, D., Yates, J. F., Simga-Mugan, C. and Oztin, S. 2003. Professional vs. amateur judgment accuracy: the case of foreign exchange rates. *Organizational Behavior and Human Decision Processes* 91, 169–185.

Peachy, R., Spiegelhalter, D. and Marteau, T. M. 2013. Impact of plain packaging of tobacco products on smoking in adults and children: an elicitation of international experts' estimates. *BMC Public Health* 13, 18.

Peel, J. 2005. *The precautionary principle in practice: environmental decision-making and scientific uncertainty*. Federation Press, Annandale, New South Wales.

Perfect, T. J. 2004. The role of self-rated ability in the accuracy of confidence judgements in eyewitness memory and general knowledge. *Applied Cognitive Psychology* 18, 157–168.

Perhac, R. M. 1998. Comparative risk assessment: where does the public fit in? *Science, Technology, and Human Values* 23, 221–241.

Pidgeon, N., Harthorn, B., Bryant, K. and Rogers-Hayden, R. 2008. Deliberating the risks of nanotechnologies for energy and health applications in the United States and United Kingdom. *Nature Nanotechnology* 4, 95–98.

Plous, S. 1993. *The psychology of judgment and decision making.* McGraw-Hill, New York.

Poff, N. L., Allan, J. D., Palmer, M. A., Hart, D. D., Richter, B. D., Arthington, A. H., Rogers, K. H., Meyer, J. L. and Stanford, J. A. 2003. River flows and water wars: emerging science for environmental decision making. *Frontiers in Ecology and the Environment* 1, 298–306.

Pons, J. M. V., Borras, J. M., Espinas, J. A., Moreno, V., Cardona, M. and Granados, A. 1999. Subjective versus statistical model assessment of mortality risk in open heart surgical procedures. *Annals of Thoracic Surgery* 67, 635–640.

Potchen, E. J. 2006. Measuring observer performance in chest radiology: some experiences. *Journal of the American College of Radiology* 3, 423–432.

Poynard, T., Munteanu, M., Ratziu, V., Benhamou, Y., Di Martino, V., Taieb, J. and Opolon, P. 2002. Truth survival in clinical research: an evidence-based requiem. *Annals of Internal Medicine* 136, 888–895.

Preston, B. J. 2003. Science and the law: evaluating evidentiary reliability. *Australian Bar Review* 23, 263–295.

Priest, G. and Thomason, N. 2007. 60% Proof. *Australasian Journal of Logic* 5, 89–100.

Punt, A. E. and Hilborn, R. 1997. Fisheries stock assessment and decision analysis: the Bayesian approach. *Reviews in Fish Biology and Fisheries* 7, 35–63.

Regan, H. M., Colyvan, M. and Burgman, M. A. 2000. A proposal for fuzzy IUCN categories and criteria. *Biological Conservation* 92, 101–108.

Regan, H. M., Colyvan, M. and Burgman, M. A. 2002. A taxonomy and treatment of uncertainty for ecology and conservation biology. *Ecological Applications* 12, 618–628.

Regan, H. M., Lupia, R., Drinnan, A. N. and Burgman, M. A. 2001. The currency and tempo of extinction. *American Naturalist* 157, 1–10.

Reischman, R. 2002. Critical care cardiovascular nurse expert and novice diagnostic cue utilization. *Journal of Advanced Nursing* 39, 24–34.

Rennie, D. and Chalmers, I. 2009. Assessing authority. *Journal of the American Medical Association* 301, 1819–1821.

Rohrmann, B. 1994. Risk perception of different societal groups: Australian findings and cross-national comparisons. *Australian Journal of Psychology* 46, 150–163.

Rohrmann, B. 1998. The risk notion: epistemological and empirical consider-
ations. In M. G. Stewart and R. E. Melchers, editors. *Integrated risk assessment*. Balkema, Rotterdam.

Rothlisberger, J. D., Lodge, D. M., Cooke, R. M. and Finnoff, D. C. 2010. Future
declines of the binational Laurentian Great Lakes fisheries: the importance of
environmental and cultural change. *Frontiers in Ecology and the Environment*
8, 239–244.

Rowe, G. and Wright, G. 2001. Expert opinions in forecasting: the role of the
Delphi technique. In J. S. Armstrong, editor. *Principles of forecasting: a handbook for researchers and practitioners*. Kluwer Academic Publishers, Boston.

Ruckelshaus, M. H., Levin, P., Johnson, J. B. and Kareiva, P. M. 2002. The Pacific
Salmon wars: what science brings to the challenge of recovering species.
Annual Review of Ecology and Systematics 33, 665–706.

Ruger, T. W., Kim, P. T., Martin, A. D. and Quinn, K. M. 2004. The Supreme
Court forecasting project: legal and political science approaches to predicting
Supreme Court decisionmaking. *Columbia Law Review* 104, 1150–1209.

Russo, J. E. and Schoemaker, P. J. H. 1992. Managing overconfidence. *Sloan
Management Review* 33, 7–17.

Savage, L. J. 1972. *The foundations of statistics*. Dover Publications, New York.

Schultz-Hardt, S., Brodbeck, F. C., Mojzisch, A., Kerschreiter, R. and Frey, D.
2006. Group decision making in hidden profile situations: dissent as a facilitator for decision quality. *Journal of Personality and Social Psychology* 91,
1080–1093.

Schultze, T., Mojzisch, A. and Schulz-Hardt, S. 2012. Why groups perform better
than individuals at quantitative judgment tasks: group-to-individual transfer as an alternative to differential weighting. *Organizational Behavior and
Human Decision Processes* 118, 24–36.

Schum, D. A. and Morris, J. R. 2007. Assessing the competence and credibility of
human sources of intelligence evidence: contributions from law and probability. *Law, Probability and Risk* 6, 247–274.

Sentz, K. and Ferson, S. 2002. Combination of evidence in Dempster-Shafer theory.
SAND Report, SAND2002-0835. Sandia National Laboratories, Albuquerque,
New Mexico.

Shaffer, M. L. 1987. Minimum viable populations: coping with uncertainty. In
M. E. Soulé, editor. *Viable populations for conservation*. Cambridge University
Press.

Shanteau, J. 1992a. Competence in experts: the role of task characteristics.
Organizational Behavior and Human Decision Processes 53, 252–266.

Shanteau, J. 1992b. How much information does an expert use? Is it relevant? *Acta Psychologica* 81, 75–86.

Shipley, B. 2000. *Cause and correlation in biology.* Cambridge University Press.

Shrader-Frechette, K. 1996a. Methodological rules for four classes of scientific uncertainty. In J. Lemons, editor. *Scientific uncertainty and environmental problem solving.* Blackwell, Cambridge, Massachusetts.

Shrader-Frechette, K. 1996b. Value judgments in verifying and validating risk assessment models. In C. R. Cothern, editor. *Handbook for environmental risk decision making: values, perceptions and ethics.* CRC Lewis Publishers, Boca Raton.

Simon, H. 1959. Theories for decision-making in economic and behavioral science. *The American Economic Review* 49, 253–283.

Slovic, P. 1999. Trust, emotion, sex, politics, and science: surveying the risk-assessment battlefield. *Risk Analysis* 19, 689–701.

Slovic, P., Fischhoff, B. and Lichtenstein, S. 1984. Perception and acceptability of risk from energy systems. In W. R. Fruendenburg and E. A. Rosa, editors. *Public reactions to nuclear power: are there critical masses?* AAAS/Westview, Boulder, Colorado.

Slovic, P., Monahan, J. and MacGregor, D. G. 2000. Violence risk assessment and risk communication: the effects of using actual cases, providing instruction, and employing probability versus frequency formats. *Law and Human Behavior* 24, 271–296.

Soll, J. B. and Klayman, J. 2004. Overconfidence in interval estimates. *Journal of Experimental Psychology: Learning, Memory, and Cognition* 30, 299.

Solomon, S., Qin, D., Manning, M., Chen, Z., Marquis, M., Averyt, K. B., Tignor, M. and Miller, H. L. 2007. *Climate Change 2007: The Physical Science Basis.* Contribution of Working Group I to the Fourth Assessment Report of the Intergovernmental Panel on Climate Change. Cambridge University Press, Cambridge and New York.

Speirs-Bridge, A., Fidler, F., McBride, M., Flander, L., Cumming, G. and Burgman, M. 2010. Reducing overconfidence in the interval judgments of experts. *Risk Analysis* 30, 512–523.

Spetzler, C. S. and Staelvonholstein, C. A. S. 1975. Probability encoding in decision analysis. *Management Science* 22, 340–358.

Spiegelhalter, D. J., Harris, N. L. and Franklin, R. C. G. 1994. Empirical evaluation of prior beliefs about frequencies: methodology and a case study in congenital heart disease. *Journal of the American Statistical Association* 89, 435–443.

Spruijt, P., Knol, A. B., Vasileiadou, E., Devilee, J., Lebret, E. and Petersen, A. C. 2014. Roles of scientists as policy advisers on complex issues: a literature review. *Environmental Science and Policy* 40, 16–25.

Stasser, G. and Titus, W. 1985. Pooling of unshared information in group decision making: biased information sampling during discussion. *Journal of Personality and Social Psychology* 48, 1467–1478.

Stephens, M. E., Goodwin, B. W. and Andres, T. H. 1993. Deriving parameter probability density functions. *Reliability Engineering and System Safety* 42, 271–291.

Stern, P. C. and Fineberg, H., editors. 1996. *Understanding risk: informing decisions in a democratic society*. National Academy Press, Washington, DC.

Sternberg, R. J., Wagner, R. K. and Okagaki, L. 1993. Practical intelligence: the nature and role of tacit knowledge in work and at school. In J. M. Puckett and H. W. Reese, editors. *Mechanisms of everyday cognition*. Lawrence Erlbaum Associates, Hillside, New Jersey.

Stewart, M. G. and Melchers, R. E. 1997. *Probabilistic risk assessment of engineering systems*. Chapman and Hall, London.

Stirling, A. 2007. A general framework for analysing diversity in science, technology and society. *Journal of the Royal Society Interface* 4, 707–719.

Stow, C. A. and Borsuk, M. E. 2003. Enhancing causal assessment of estuarine fishkills using graphical models. *Ecosystems* 6, 11–19.

Surowiecki, J. 2005. *The wisdom of crowds: why the many are smarter than the few and how collective wisdom shapes business, economies, societies and nations*. Doubleday, New York.

Taylor, S. E. and Brown, J. D. 1988. Illusion and well-being: a social psychological perspective on mental health. *Psychological Bulletin* 103, 193–210.

Teigen, K. H. and Jørgensen, M. 2005. When 90% confidence intervals are 50% certain: on the credibility of credible intervals. *Applied Cognitive Psychology* 19, 455–475.

Tetlock, P. E. 2005. *Expert political opinion, how good is it? How can we know?* Princeton University Press, New Jersey.

Tetlock, P. E. and Mellers, B. A. 2011. Intelligent management of intelligence agencies. *American Psychologist* 66, 542–554.

Thaler, R. H. 1991. *Quasi-rational economics*. Russell Sage Foundation, New York.

Todd, P. M. and Gigerenzer, G. 2007. Environments that make us smart. *Current Directions in Psychological Science* 16, 167–171.

Toulmin, S. 1958. *The uses of argument*. Cambridge University Press.

Tufte, E. 1997. *Visual explanations: images and quantities, evidence and narrative*. Graphics Press, Cheshire, Connecticut.

Tversky, A. and Kahneman, D. 1971. Belief in the law of small numbers. *Psychological Bulletin* 76, 105–110.

Tversky, A. and Kahneman, D. 1974. Judgement under uncertainty: heuristics and biases. *Science* 185, 1124–1131.

Tversky, A. and Kahneman, D. 1985. The framing of decisions and the psychology of choice. In G. Wright, editor. *Behavioral decision making*, pp. 25–41. Springer, New York.

Tversky, A. and Kahneman, D. 1982a. Belief in the law of small numbers. In D. Kahneman, P. Slovic and A. Tversky, editors. *Judgement under uncertainty: heuristics and biases*. Cambridge University Press, pp. 23–30.

Tversky, A. and Kahneman, D. 1982b. Causal schemata in judgments under uncertainty. In D. Kahneman, P. Slovic, A. Tversky, editors. *Judgment under uncertainty: heuristics and biases*. Cambridge University Press.

Ulery, B. T., Hicklin, R. A., Buscaglia, J. and Roberts, M. A. 2011. Accuracy and reliability of forensic latent fingerprint decisions. *Proceedings of the National Academy of Sciences of the USA* 108, 7733–7738.

Valverde, L. J. 2001. Expert judgment resolution in technically-intensive policy disputes. In I. Linkov and J. Palma-Oliveira, editors. *Assessment and management of environmental risks*. Kluwer Academic Publishers, Dordrecht.

Van der Heijden, K. 1996. *Scenarios: the art of strategic conversation*. Wiley, Chichester.

van Frassen, B. 1984. Belief and the will. *Journal of Philosophy* 81, 235–256.

van Gelder, T. 2013. *Argument mapping*. In H. Pashler, editor. *Encyclopedia of the mind*. Sage, Thousand Oaks, CA.

Vanackere, G. 1999. Minimizing ambiguity and paraconsistency. *Logique et analyse* 165, 39–160.

Veatch, R. M. 1991. Consensus of expertise: the role of consensus of experts in formulating public policy and estimating facts. *Journal of Medicine and Philosophy* 16, 427–445.

Verran, H. 2002. Transferring strategies of land management: indigenous land owners and environmental scientists. *Research in Science and Technology Studies, Knowledge and Society* 13, 155–181.

Vose, D. 1996. *Quantitative risk analysis: a guide to Monte Carlo simulation modelling*. Wiley, Chichester.

Wade, P. R. 2000. Bayesian methods in conservation biology. *Conservation Biology* 14, 1308–1316.

Wagenaar, W. A. and Keren, G. B. 1986. Does the expert know? The reliability of predictions and confidence ratings of experts. In E. H. Hollnagel, G. Mancini and D. D. Woods, editors. *Intelligent decision support in process environments*. Springer-Verlag, Berlin.

Walley, P. 1991. *Statistical reasoning with imprecise probabilities*. Chapman and Hall, London.

Walley, P. 2000. Towards a unified theory of imprecise probability. *International Journal of Approximate Reasoning* 24, 125–148.

Walley, P. and De Cooman, G. 2001. A behavioral model for linguistic uncertainty. *Information Sciences* 134, 1–37.

Wallsten, T. S. and Budescu, D. V. 1983. Encoding subjective probabilities: a psychological and psychometric review. *Management Science* 29, 151–173.

Wallsten, T. S., Budescu, D. V., Erev, I. and Diederich, A. 1997. Evaluating and combining subjective probability estimates. *Journal of Behavioral Decision Making* 10, 243–268.

Walton, D. 1997. *Appeal to expert opinion: arguments from authority.* Pennsylvania State University Press, University Park.

Weber, E. U., Blais, A.-R., and Betz, N. E. 2002. A domain-specific risk-attitude scale: measuring risk perceptions and risk behaviors. *Journal of Behavioral Decision Making* 15, 263–290.

Webler, T., Levine, D., Rakel, H. and Renn, O. 1991. A novel approach to reducing uncertainty: the Delphi group. *Technological Forecasting and Social Change* 39, 253–263.

Weiss, D. J. and Shanteau, J. 2012. Decloaking the privileged expert. *Journal of Management and Organization* 18, 300–310.

Welke, K. F., O'Brien, S. M., Peterson, E. D., Ungerleider, R. M., Jacobs, M. L. and Jacobs, J. P. 2009. The complex relationship between pediatric cardiac surgical case volumes and mortality rates in a national clinical database. *Journal of Thoracic and Cardiovascular Surgery* 137, 1133–1140.

Windschitl, P. D. 2002. Judging the accuracy of a likelihood judgment: the case of smoking risk. *Journal of Behavioral Decision Making* 15, 19–35.

Winkler, R. L. and Poses, R. M. 1993. Evaluating and combining physicians' probabilities of survival in an intensive care unit. *Management Science* 39, 1526–1543.

Wintle, B. C. 2013. Making Decisions When Estimates Conflict: Improving Judgements in Environmental Science. PhD Thesis, University of Melbourne.

Wintle, B., Mascaro, M., Fidler, F., McBride, M., Burgman, M., Flander, L., Saw, G., Twardy, C., Lyon, A. and Manning, B. 2012. The intelligence game: assessing Delphi groups and structured question formats. In J. Corkill, M. Coole and C. Valli, editors. *Proceedings of the 5th Australian Security and Intelligence Conference.* pp. 14–26. Security Research Institute, Edith Cowan University.

Wintle, B. C., Fidler, F. M. and Burgman, M. A. 2013b. The trial of scientists at L'Aquila: Lessons for risk communication. *Risk Analysis* (in review).

Wise, G. 1976. The accuracy of technological forecasts, 1890–1940. *Futures* 8, 411–419.

WMD Commission. 2005. The commission on the intelligence capabilities of the United States regarding weapons of mass destruction. March 31, 2005. *US Government* 374. In Wheaton, K. and Chido, D. 2007. Evaluating Intelligence. *Competitive Intelligence Magazine* 10, 2–19.

Wolfgang, P. 2002. Witness 'conferencing'. *Arbitration International* 18, 47–58.

Woolley, A. W., Chabris, C. F., Pentland, A., Hashmi, N. and Malone, T. W. 2010. Evidence for a collective intelligence factor in the performance of human groups. *Science* 330, 686–688.

Wright, G., Bolger, F. and Rowe, G. 2002. An empirical test of the relative validity of expert and lay judgments of risk. *Risk Analysis* 22, 1107–1122.

Wynne, B. 1996. May the sheep safely graze? A reflexive view of the expert-lay knowledge divide. In S. Lash, B. Szerszynski and B. Wynne, editors. *Risk, environment and modernity: towards a new ecology*. Sage Publications, London.

Yearley, S. 2000. Making systematic sense of public discontents with expert knowledge: two analytical approaches and a case study. *Public Understanding of Science* 9, 105–122.

Zadeh, L. A. 1986. A simple view of the Dempster–Shafer theory of evidence and its implication for the rule of combination. *The AI Magazine* 1986, 85–90.

Index

Made in United States
North Haven, CT
12 June 2023

37660710R00117